EXTREME DIALOGUE

*Transform Your Words Into Wins:
Master the Art of Manifestation*

Gianna Fiecoat

*To my mother,
who taught me you can't unring a bell.*

CONTENTS

Title Page
Dedication
Preface
Chapter 1: Fusion of Worlds — 1
Chapter 2: Beyond Positivity — 8
Chapter 3: The Pillars of Progress — 17
Chapter 4: The Blueprint of Success — 24
Chapter 5: Reinventing Self-Improvement — 33
Chapter 6: Unleashing Potential — 41
Chapter 7: New Horizons in 'Self-Help' — 48
Chapter 8: Amplifying Impact — 55
Chapter 9: The Analytical Mind — 62
Chapter 10: A Self-Improvement Enthusiasts Guide to Actionable Reality — 69
Chapter 11: The Data-Driven Professional's Blueprint — 76
Chapter 12: The Progressive Mentor & Educator — 84
Chapter 13: Consciously Creating Familial bonds — 93
Chapter 14: The Transformative Journey — 99
Epilogue — 106

PREFACE

"The way to get started is to quit talking and begin doing." - Walt Disney

※ ※ ※

At the very heart of *From Dialogue to Reality*, lies the powerful conviction that the bridge between conversation and action is not just traversable but, indeed, the foundation for all tangible success. This book is designed to be a beacon for the young professionals and entrepreneurs who, despite being steeped in a world brimming with information, find themselves stranded on the shores of actualization, unable to turn the tide of their dreams into reality.

In the following pages, you will embark on a transformative journey through the innovative method of "Extreme Dialogue." This approach is neither a fleeting trend nor a shallow promise but a meticulously designed framework grounded in the principles of growth hacking, strategic communication, and data-driven decision making. It's about elevating your words beyond mere intention, turning them into your most powerful tools for crafting the life and career you've envisioned.

The inception of this book was not an accident. It came from observing countless talented individuals around me, people who could articulate their dreams with utmost clarity yet struggled to translate these visions into the fabric of their daily lives. I saw echoes of this dilemma in forums, coaching sessions, and even in reflective moments with peers. This pervasive gap between ideation and implementation became the catalyst for "From Dialogue to Reality."

Within these stories, I recognized a consistent theme: the absence of a structured approach to bring one's internal narrative into alignment with external actions. It became apparent that what is often dismissed as the 'soft' skills of effective communication, accountability, and strategic dialogue are actually the most critical tools in our arsenal for achieving tangible results.

This journey has been enriched immeasurably by the insights of thought leaders across disciplines of PR, branding, and marketing. The contributions from mentors and peers who championed the importance of genuine relationships and transparent communication have been indispensable. Their collective wisdom underscores the entire narrative of this book, emphasizing that success is not a solo endeavor but the triumph of collaboration and shared vision.

To each one of you investing your time and energy into these pages, I extend my deepest gratitude. Recognizing the multitude of options at your fingertips, your decision to explore the potential of "Extreme Dialogue" with me is an honor. This book is an invitation to not just dream, but to dare—to convert your strategic conversations into the wins you've only spoken of.

The ideal reader for this narrative is someone at the nexus of professional ambition and personal growth, eager to leverage the rich data and evidence-based practices from their work life into more personal domains such as fulfillment and self-improvement. No prior expertise in the fields of PR, marketing, or growth hacking is required, just an open mind and the readiness to engage with your aspirations in a radically new way.

Thank you for choosing to embark on this journey with me. Let's dive in, and together, transform our dialogues into the reality we seek.

CHAPTER 1: FUSION OF WORLDS

When Analytics Meets Aspiration

Could the melding of data with desire truly present a path to a life abundant with both meaning and method?

Unlock the Power of Extreme Dialogue

Extreme Dialogue represents a groundbreaking approach, merging analytical rigor with the human dream of personal growth. In today's dynamic landscape, this fusion is not just innovative; it's necessary. Traditional personal development methods often operate on the fringes of either too abstract or purely motivational realms. They may fuel temporary enthusiasm but frequently fail to deliver lasting transformation. However, Extreme Dialogue stands poised to bridge this gap, offering a roadmap for translating personal and professional aspirations into tangible success. This chapter unveils how combining data-driven strategies with personal aspirations sets the stage for achieving unprecedented growth.

At its core, Extreme Dialogue harnesses the strength of analytical thinking to inform and guide the pursuit of personal growth dreams. The method deploys metrics, analysis, and pragmatic strategies typically reserved for fields like growth hacking and marketing strategy. Imagine applying these tools, known for transforming businesses and products, to personal growth. Such an approach offers clarity, removing the guesswork and enabling a more targeted pursuit of goals. **Understanding the blend between analytics and aspiration is the first step** towards mastering the ability to manifest one's dreams into reality with precision and insight.

Traditional personal development methodologies often provide a one-size-fits-all solution, which may not resonate with everyone. **Individuals with a predisposed analytical mindset might find these methods lack the structure and specificity they crave.** Extreme Dialogue fills this gap by introducing a structured yet flexible framework that respects the uniqueness of individual aspirations while employing a data-driven approach to measure progress. This methodical approach not only motivates but also equips individuals with the tools to navigate their growth journey effectively.

The impact of this fusion between the analytical and aspirational realms cannot be overstated. By adopting a structured approach, individuals learn not just to dream but to strategically map out their path to achievement. It translates lofty ambitions into actionable steps, grounded in data and real-world applicability. This transition from abstract goals to concrete results embodies the essence of Extreme Dialogue. It's about making informed decisions that propel you toward your objectives, leveraging insights derived from a meticulous analysis of one's actions, outcomes, and the environment.

Furthermore, Extreme Dialogue promotes **collaboration and transparency** in the pursuit of personal growth. By fostering genuine relationships built on trust and openness, individuals can leverage collective wisdom to accelerate their journey towards success. This aligns with the importance of teamwork and collaborative efforts in achieving notable advancements, whether in personal or professional arenas.

The method also emphasizes innovation and creative thinking. Encouraging individuals to think outside the box, Extreme

Dialogue integrates intellectual curiosity with a strategic framework to explore new growth avenues. This blend nurtures a mindset that is continually seeking better, more efficient ways to achieve goals, applying the principles of continuous improvement not just to professional projects but to personal development as well.

This chapter sets the stage for the transformative journey that Extreme Dialogue offers. It lays down the foundational concepts necessary for understanding how this unique approach can lead to tangible successes. As we progress through the book, we'll delve deeper into specific strategies and case studies that illustrate the power of this methodology. By engaging with Extreme Dialogue, readers will learn how to strategically transform their words into wins, mastering the art of manifestation without the frustration of unmet expectations. Through this lens, we embark on a journey to bridge the gap between a positive mindset and tangible outcomes, empowering readers to unlock a level of personal fulfillment previously thought unattainable.

Comprehend How Extreme Dialogue Blends Analytical Thinking with Personal Growth Dreams

Extreme Dialogue represents an innovative merging point where the precision of analytics meets the fluidity of personal aspirations. In a world increasingly driven by data, the emphasis on analytical thinking has traversed beyond the confines of professional environments, cementing its importance in personal growth strategies. Yet, the alignment of this analytical rigor with the often nebulous nature of personal dreams may seem counterintuitive at first.

Imagine your aspirations as a vibrant, abstract painting, full of potential but lacking in structure. In comes analytical thinking, much like a skilled artist who adds definition and clarity without compromising the painting's inherent beauty. This symbiosis does not dilute the essence of personal dreams but rather provides a framework through which they can be more effectively pursued and realized.

The scope of analytics, traditionally seen as cold and impersonal, surprisingly suits the realm of personal development when applied correctly. Metrics, data analysis, and structured thinking help in setting clear, attainable goals out of abstract desires. It lays down a path that is measurable and, most importantly, actionable. The clarity derived from this approach enables individuals to make informed decisions, track their progress, and adjust their strategies as needed, keeping their aspirations not just as distant dreams but as goals within reach.

The fear that integrating analytics into personal growth could strip away its human element is unfounded. Rather, it enriches the journey by embedding evidence-based milestones along the way. Each step taken is informed, intentional, and resonates with the individual's core aspirations, making the pursuit of personal growth both a science and an art.

The key point is to appreciate how Extreme Dialogue harmoniously blends the structured world of analytics with the fluid domain of personal aspirations, making the pursuit of dreams more tangible and achievable.

Identifying Gaps in Traditional Personal Development Methods

Traditional personal development methods often resemble a well-meant pep talk that, while uplifting, lacks specificity and actionable insights. These methods encourage individuals to dream big and strive for improvement but fall short on providing a clear roadmap on how to navigate the journey from aspirations to reality. The general advice dispensed tends to be broad, leaving individuals to decipher the 'how' on their own.

Here, Extreme Dialogue steps in to fill the void. By combining the rigour of analytics with the soul-stirring call of personal dreams, it bridges the gap between abstract aspirations and tangible achievements. It recognizes the critical need for measurable steps and structured strategies — elements often overlooked in traditional approaches.

Imagine navigating a foreign city without a map or GPS. The exploration, though exciting, is inefficacious and possibly fruitless if you have specific destinations in mind. Extreme Dialogue, in contrast, equips you with the navigational tools — analytics akin to your GPS — directing you towards your desired outcomes with precision and clarity.

At the heart of its philosophy, Extreme Dialogue emphasizes the importance of setting quantifiable goals, leveraging data for informed decision-making, and systematically tracking progress. This methodical approach demystifies the journey toward personal and professional development, making success less about luck and more about strategic action.

Moreover, Extreme Dialogue fosters a deeper understanding and engagement with one's personal growth journey. It encourages critical thinking and self-reflection, enabling individuals to refine their aspirations and align them with realistic, actionable plans. This involvement not only increases the likelihood of achieving set goals but also enhances the overall journey toward self-improvement.

Could this fusion of analytics with personal development be the missing link in transforming aspirations into attainable goals?

Understanding the Impact of a Structured Approach to Translating Dreams into Tangible Outcomes

The implementation of a structured approach to personal growth, as endorsed by Extreme Dialogue, serves as a powerful catalyst for turning dreams into reality. This method revolves around the application of analytical tools and data-driven decision-making to the realm of personal and professional development. Recognizing and harnessing the power of this structured approach can significantly amplify one's ability to achieve desired outcomes.

Imagine building a bridge where each plank represents a step towards your goal. Without a clear plan and understanding of where each plank goes, building a stable bridge would be nearly impossible. Extreme Dialogue acts as the architect, providing not only the blueprint but also the best practice methods and measurements for placing each plank, ensuring that every step taken is secure and propels you forward.

This approach is not just about setting goals but about identifying the most efficient routes to achieve them. It involves a continuous cycle of planning, action, evaluation, and adjustment. By applying analytics, individuals can set benchmarks, track progress in real-time, and pivot strategies based on concrete data rather than intuition alone.

The structured path laid out by Extreme Dialogue empowers individuals by providing clarity amidst the chaos. It transforms vague aspirations into specific, actionable objectives, effectively removing the guesswork from personal development. The certainty this method offers leads to increased motivation, as individuals are no longer navigating in the dark but are guided by tangible milestones and achievements.

Extreme Dialogue successfully merges analytical thought processes with the pursuit of personal aspirations, filling the gaps left by traditional personal development methods, and providing a tangible framework for achieving dreams. It transforms the abstract into the actionable, making success not just a possibility but a predictable outcome.

In this chapter, we've delved into the powerful fusion of

analytical thinking with personal growth aspirations. Extreme Dialogue offers a unique pathway that bridges the gap between the structured approach of data-driven professions and the heartfelt dreams of individuals seeking personal and professional transformation. By exploring the limitations of traditional personal development methods and showcasing how **Extreme Dialogue** fills these gaps, we've provided a glimpse into a groundbreaking approach that can revolutionize the way you manifest your aspirations into reality.

As you embark on this journey of discovery through the upcoming chapters, **brace yourself for a transformational experience** that will empower you to unlock your full potential. Get ready to shatter preconceived boundaries and unleash a new realm of possibilities in your personal and professional life. Through the lens of **Extreme Dialogue**, you will not only gain valuable insights on how to translate your dreams into actionable steps but also cultivate a mindset that embraces both data-driven strategies and personal growth aspirations.

Your future success story awaits as we navigate through the realms of dialogue, aspiration, and action, sculpting a narrative that embodies collaboration, innovation, and tangible results. The pages to come are packed with strategies, insights, and tools designed to propel you towards your goals with precision and purpose. Stay engaged, stay motivated, and get ready to witness the fusion of worlds as **Extreme Dialogue** unravels the essence of what it means to thrive in a data-savvy, goal-oriented world.

CHAPTER 2: BEYOND POSITIVITY

The Power of Intentional Language and the art of manifestation.

Unleashing the Full Spectrum of Success Through Extreme Dialogue

In a world saturated with the doctrine of positive thinking, the proposition that sheer optimism isn't the golden ticket to actualizing one's ambitions might seem controversial. However, it's imperative to understand that while maintaining a positive outlook is beneficial, it's the precision and intentionality behind our language and communication that truly molds our reality. **Extreme Dialogue** pushes beyond the boundaries of positive psychology, advocating for a balanced amalgamation of positive mindset with strategic and intentional use of language to craft the life and success we fervently aspire to.

The essence of **intentional language** and communication as a tool for manifestation is often overlooked in the traditional discourse on positive thinking. This chapter delves deep into the mechanics of how our words not only represent our thoughts but actively shape our experiences and interactions with the world. Words carry power - the power to heal, to build, to manifest, and equally, to destroy and repel. It's this power that Extreme Dialogue seeks to harness through a methodical approach to communication, ensuring that every word spoken or written aligns with one's core intentions and manifestation objectives.

Exploring the limitations of positive thinking in manifesting outcomes reveals the stark reality that optimism without action and precise communication is akin to a rudderless ship. It's not enough to simply 'think positive'; one must also communicate positively, with intention and clarity. This chapter sheds light on the **nuanced role** that language plays in not only shaping our thoughts but in creating a tangible impact on our reality.

Understanding the importance of language and communication in shaping reality is pivotal. Every conversation, every piece of written communication, and even our internal dialogue are brush strokes in the grand canvas of our lives. The shift towards employing **intentional language** is not merely about choosing positivity over negativity; it's about choosing words that explicitly align with our goals, aspirations, and the reality we wish to manifest.

Communicating with Intention for Manifestation

Step 1: Practice Mindfulness in Language

Awareness is the first step towards transformation. Observing and subsequently adjusting your language to ensure it reflects positivity and empowerment sets a solid foundation. This extends beyond avoiding negativity to actively infusing your daily dialogue with words that support your aspirations.

Step 2: Use Affirmations

Affirmations are potent tools for reshaping your subconscious narrative. Regularly engaging with affirmations that resonate with your intentions enhances your belief system and propels you towards your goals.

Step 3: Practice Active Listening

Active listening enriches your communication skills, allowing for more meaningful interactions. It fosters empathy and understanding, vital components for nurturing relationships that support your journey towards success.

Step 4: Choose Words that Align with Your Intentions

Intentional language means selecting words with precision, words that resonate with your goals and intentions, thereby reinforcing your path to manifestation.

Step 5: Visualize Positive Outcomes

Visualizing the successful outcome of your words adds a layer of potency to your communication. This practice aligns your verbal and mental frequencies, amplifying the manifestation process.

Step 6: Practice Gratitude in Communication

Integrating gratitude into your everyday conversations not only shifts your perspective towards positivity but also attracts more reasons to be grateful, thereby enhancing the manifestation of your intentions.

Step 7: Use Empowering Questions

Shifting the narrative from victimhood to empowerment through strategic questioning opens up new possibilities and enables solution-oriented thinking, a critical aspect of successful manifestation.

Step 8: Choose Empowering Responses

Facing adversities with resilience and empowered language demonstrates a commitment to overcoming obstacles and further solidifies your path towards achieving your goals.

Step 9: Reflect and Adjust

Continuous reflection on your communication patterns and making necessary adjustments ensures that your language remains aligned with your intentions, enhancing your manifestation efforts.

Through diligent practice of these steps, the journey from dialogue to reality becomes not just a possibility, but an impending certainty. The transformation from positive thinking to **intentional language** and communication is a powerful tool in the arsenal of anyone looking to manifest their dreams into reality. It underscores the importance of not just what we think, but critically, how we express those thoughts to the world. This chapter serves as a blueprint for making every word count, turning dialogue into a strategic instrument of manifestation and, ultimately, unlocking tangible success.

Exploring the Limitations of Positive Thinking in Manifesting Outcomes

Positive thinking is often heralded as a miracle cure for life's challenges, a silver bullet promising success and fulfillment with little more than a sunny outlook. This perspective, however, while beneficial in fostering optimism, has its limitations when not supported by action. Positive thinking serves as a foundation, encouraging us to aim high, but it requires more to manifest tangible results.

Imagine for a moment a gardener who believes in the beauty of their garden but never waters the plants. No matter how positive the gardener's outlook, without the action of watering, the garden will not flourish. This analogy illustrates the fundamental truth that positive thinking must be paired with purposeful actions to achieve desired outcomes.

Moreover, research in the field of positive psychology suggests that while optimism can enhance our mental health, it does not guarantee the achievement of our objectives. A vital aspect often overlooked in the discourse on positive thinking is the specificity and intention behind our thoughts and actions. It is not enough to simply have a positive outlook; we must direct this positivity with intention towards well-defined goals.

This specificity and intentionality in our approach shift the focus from a vague positivity to a more grounded and practical strategy for realizing our dreams. In essence, while positive thinking opens the door to possibilities, it is the clarity and purpose of our actions that invite success into our lives.

In summary, though positive thinking creates a conducive mindset for success, without specific, intentional actions, it alone cannot manifest desired outcomes.

Communicating with Intention for Manifestation

The way we communicate, not just with others but with ourselves, profoundly influences our reality. Words are powerful; they can both create and destroy, lift us up or pull us down. Recognizing the power of language and communication is the first step in reshaping our reality to align with our aspirations.

Imagine language as the paint with which we color our world. Negative, self-limiting words inject our canvas with dark hues, creating a world that reflects those very limitations. Conversely, positive, empowering language fills our canvas with light, painting a world brimming with possibility and success. This metaphor underscores the transformative impact of intentional communication on our reality.

Communicating with Intention for Manifestation

Step 1: Practice Mindfulness in Language

Become aware of the language you use daily. Notice any negative or self-limiting phrases and consciously replace them with positive and empowering words. This shift transforms your self-dialogue and the narrative of your life.

Step 2: Use Affirmations

Incorporate affirmations into your routine. Choose statements that resonate with your intentions and repeat them often. Whether written or spoken, affirmations rewire your brain, fostering positive beliefs that support your goals.

Step 3: Practice Active Listening

Engage in conversations with full attention. Active listening enhances understanding, deepens connections, and enriches communication, supporting your manifestation journey.

Step 4: Choose Words that Align with Your Intentions

Select words that mirror your desired outcomes. By articulating your challenges as opportunities, you shift your perspective, fostering resilience and determination.

Step 5: Visualize Positive Outcomes

As you speak, envision the successful realization of your words. This visualization strengthens the link between your language and your intentions, enhancing the manifestation process.

Step 6: Practice Gratitude in Communication

Integrate gratitude into your interactions. Acknowledging the positive fosters a supportive mindset, essential for manifesting your desires.

Step 7: Use Empowering Questions

Shift your internal dialogue through empowering questions. This reframing opens up new pathways for creative and solution-oriented thinking.

Step 8: Choose Empowering Responses

Face challenges with empowering language. Responding with resilience and resourcefulness transforms obstacles into stepping stones toward your goals.

Step 9: Reflect and Adjust

Continuously assess and refine your communication. Awareness and adaptation are key to aligning your language with your manifestations.

How might shifting your language transform your reality?

Learn How to Employ Intentional Language to Support Manifestation Goals

Intentional language serves as a bridge between thought and manifestation, transforming abstract desires into tangible realities. It's not merely about choosing positive words but about embedding these words with the power of intention. This process aligns our verbal expressions with our deepest desires, creating a vibrational match that attracts what we seek into our lives.

Imagine your words as seeds planted in the fertile ground of the universe. Intentional language ensures that these seeds are watered with purpose, nurtured by positive thoughts, and supported by specific actions. Just as seeds require the right conditions to grow, our dreams need the proper linguistic environment to flourish.

Employing intentional language requires mindfulness and practice. It starts with a shift in perspective, viewing every word as a building block in the construction of our reality. By choosing words that reflect our aspirations, we set the framework for our thoughts, attitudes, and actions to align with our goals.

This conscious cultivation of our spoken and thought language is not a one-time effort but a continuous process. It involves recognizing the impact of our words, refining our choices, and aligning our language with our vision of success. Through intentional language, we direct our energy towards what we want to manifest, opening the avenues of possibility and making our dreams accessible.

By exploring the limitations of positive thinking, discovering the importance of intentional language, and learning how to employ it, we unlock the full potential of our words to transform reality.

Positive thinking serves as a crucial foundation for success, but alone, it may not be sufficient to bring your goals into reality. This chapter has illuminated the vital role that intentional language and communication play in the manifestation process. **By exploring the limitations of positive thinking, highlighting the importance of language in shaping our reality, and learning how to employ intentional language to support our manifestation goals**, we have unlocked a powerful key to achieving tangible success.

Remember, the way we communicate with ourselves and others is not mere chatter; it is the building blocks of our reality. Every word we utter carries weight in the creation of our future outcomes. Let this knowledge urge you to be deliberate and mindful in your conversations, both internally and externally. **Harness the power of intentional language to direct your thoughts, words, and actions towards the manifestation of your deepest desires.**

As you move forward, keep in mind that a positive mindset, intentional language, and effective communication are a trifecta for transformation. Do not underestimate the impact of your words and the power they hold in co-creating your reality. Challenge the misconception that mere positivity can bring success and, instead, embrace the nuanced interplay of thoughts, words, and actions in manifesting your dreams.

Let this understanding be your guide as you navigate the

path from dialogue to reality. Your words have the potential to shape the world around you, so choose them wisely. Embrace intentional language as a vehicle for transformation and watch as your intentions materialize into tangible victories. The journey from dialogue to reality is yours to command.

CHAPTER 3: THE PILLARS OF PROGRESS

Merging Mindset with Method

The Unseen Blueprint for Personal Success

The journey toward self-improvement and tangible success is complex, yet attainable when approached with the right mindset and methodologies. At its core, Extreme Dialogue represents a convergence of intentional living, cognitive behavioral therapy (CBT), and manifestation techniques. This powerful trifecta is not merely about changing how we speak, but about transforming our approach to life itself. **It's about crafting a thoughtful and proactive path** that aligns our deepest aspirations with our daily actions, thereby turning dialogue into reality.

Understanding how Extreme Dialogue incorporates intentional living and cognitive behavioral therapy is foundational to mastering this approach. Intentional living urges us to lead our lives with purpose and consciousness, making decisions that are in harmony with our core values and long-term objectives. Meanwhile, CBT helps us to identify and challenge distorted thought patterns, enabling us to shift towards more positive and productive behaviors. **Together, they provide a robust framework** for personal growth, ensuring that our mindset and actions are consistently aligned with the outcomes we seek.

Manifestation techniques add another dimension to this equation, offering a method to actively bring our desires into existence. It's not about wishful thinking; it's about setting clear intentions, cultivating a positive mindset, and taking concrete steps towards our goals. **By actively visualizing and working towards what we want**, we harness the power of our thoughts and actions to shape our reality. This chapter aims to demystify these techniques, showing how to seamlessly integrate them into our daily lives for maximum effect.

The benefits of this holistic approach are multifold and profound. By combining mindset, behavior, and communication, we not only enhance our personal development but also improve our interactions with others. This alignment creates a synergy that propels us towards our goals, making success not just a possibility, but a predictable outcome. **It's about transforming potential into actuality**, leveraging every aspect of our being towards the achievement of our dreams.

Assessing the benefits of this comprehensive strategy, it's clear that Extreme Dialogue isn't merely a tool for personal advancement; it's a roadmap for living a fulfilled and impactful life. It encourages us to be architects of our own destiny, meticulously designing each day to bring us closer to our ultimate objectives. It fosters growth, resilience, and a profound sense of clarity that guides us through life's challenges with grace and determination.

Moreover, this approach emphasizes the power of teamwork and collaboration, underscoring the importance of building genuine relationships rooted in trust and transparency. Whether in personal or professional settings, **communication is key to unlocking our full potential**, bridging the gap between where we are and where we aspire to be. By fostering meaningful connections, we amplify our ability to achieve collective success, sharing the journey towards personal and shared aspirations.

In essence, the pillars of progress outlined in this chapter offer more than just a theory for success; they provide practical, actionable strategies that can be applied in everyday scenarios. They invite us to embark on a journey of self-discovery and intentional action, equipping us with the tools needed to transform our dialogue into the reality we envision. **It's a call to action** — to master the art of manifestation, to live intentionally, and to leverage the transformative power of our thoughts and behaviors in pursuit of our ultimate life goals.

Extreme Dialogue merges intentional living with cognitive behavioral therapy (CBT) to create a powerful tool for personal development. Intentional living encourages individuals to make choices aligned with their core values and goals, focusing on what truly matters to them. This method of living requires mindfulness and awareness, pushing individuals to actively design their lives rather than merely drifting through on autopilot. It's about making every decision count, whether it's how you spend your morning, the job you choose, or the relationships you nurture.

In comparison, cognitive behavioral therapy is a structured approach that identifies negative thought patterns and behaviors, aiming to transform them into positive outcomes. It operates on the principle that our thoughts, feelings, and behaviors are interconnected, suggesting that by changing one, we can influence the others. Here, the dialogue with oneself becomes critical, as it involves monitoring and challenging one's thoughts and beliefs, emphasizing the reflective aspect of intentional living.

Imagine navigating a dense forest. Intentional living serves as the compass, guiding you in the direction of your values and goals. In tandem, cognitive behavioral therapy acts as the machete, clearing away the underbrush of negative thoughts that obstruct your path. Together, they ensure not only that you're heading in the right direction but also that you're able to move forward, transforming the journey into a deliberate stride towards success.

At the core of Extreme Dialogue is the synthesis of these two strategies, ensuring that individuals don't just dream about the future they want but also pave a clear path towards it. By marrying the goal-oriented nature of intentional living with the practical, hands-on approach of CBT, Extreme Dialogue fosters a mindset geared towards action and tangible results. It's about creating a life that's not only envisioned but also meticulously crafted and realized.

The essence of the first learning objective is to harness the power of both intentional living and cognitive behavioral therapy to create a proactive and purpose-driven approach to life.

Mastering the integration of manifestation techniques into daily life is like cultivating a garden. Just as a gardener plants seeds, tends to them regularly, and patiently waits for them to grow, individuals can plant the seeds of their desires through visualization and affirmations. However, it's the consistent action and nurturing—watering these seeds with positive thoughts, gratitude, and steps towards goals—that eventually brings the garden of dreams to fruition. Manifestation isn't about wishing upon a star; it's about marrying intent with action.

Manifestation techniques, such as visualization and affirmations, encourage a mindset of abundance and possibility. By focusing on specific desires and positive outcomes, individuals can align their thoughts and energy with their goals, attracting opportunities and motivating action. It's a principle rooted in the belief that by visualizing what you want, you're more likely to recognize and seize the opportunities that will make it a reality.

Yet, integration into daily life is where many stumble. It's not merely about setting aside time for these practices but weaving them into the fabric of everyday life. For instance, using affirmations as a tool for self-encouragement during challenging moments or visualizing success as a means to maintain focus and enthusiasm.

The key is consistency. Much like watering a plant sporadically won't yield a healthy growth, sporadic manifestation practices won't yield tangible results. The integration of manifestation techniques into daily life necessitates a routine—a dedicated effort to constantly align your thoughts and actions with your desires.

Think of your daily routine as a series of dominos. Each action, each thought, is a domino, and when aligned correctly, they lead to the actualization of your goals. The magic happens not in the setup but in the consistent effort of pushing the first domino and watching the chain reaction unfold.

Can integrating manifestation techniques into your daily life be the secret bridge between dreaming and achieving?

A holistic approach that combines mindset, behavior, and communication is akin to a three-legged stool. Each leg supports the structure, ensuring stability and function. Similarly, intertwining mindset with behavior and communication fosters a robust foundation for personal growth and success. Mindset provides the beliefs and attitudes necessary for growth, behavior encompasses the actions taken towards achieving goals, and communication is the tool for expressing needs, desires, and establishing connections with others.

This comprehensive method underscores the importance of aligning thoughts, actions, and words. An optimistic mindset without the corresponding behaviors and effective communication is like a car with a powerful engine but flat tires. It has potential, but it lacks the means to move forward. Similarly, positive behavior and communication without the right mindset won't lead to sustainable change, as the underlying beliefs and attitudes aren't in sync with the outward actions.

Incorporating a holistic approach allows individuals to address obstacles comprehensively. When mindset, behavior, and communication are harmonized, obstacles become easier to navigate. Challenges in one area can often be mitigated or solved by strengths in another, providing a dynamic and flexible framework for personal development.

Flexibility is key. As individuals evolve, so too will their balance of mindset, behavior, and communication. It's not about finding a perfect balance but about adjusting the ratios as needed to support growth and success. This holistic perspective ensures that growth in one area reinforces and catalyzes growth in the others, leading to a more resilient and adaptable individual.

Merging mindset with method isn't just beneficial; it's foundational for anyone looking to deeply engage with personal growth. By embracing intentional living, cognitive behavioral therapy, and integrating manifestation techniques, individuals can craft a comprehensive roadmap towards success. This holistic approach not only aligns thoughts, actions, and words but also empowers individuals to navigate their journeys with clarity, purpose, and resilience.

Embracing a Holistic Approach

The fusion of intentional living, cognitive behavioral therapy, and manifestation techniques into Extreme Dialogue leads to a holistic approach that can revolutionize the way individuals drive personal growth. **By understanding the significance of mindset, behavior, and communication**, you pave the way for transformative change in your life. This comprehensive integration brings about a synergy that propels you towards your goals with purpose and clarity.

Integrating for Success

Mastering the art of merging mindset with method is not just a theory; it's a practical strategy for success. As you internalize the principles of intentional living, cognitive behavioral therapy, and manifestation techniques, you'll find yourself equipped with a powerful toolkit to navigate life's challenges and opportunities.

Through this synergy, you lay the foundation for a future built on intentionality, resilience, and growth.

Building Your Path to Success

As you navigate the terrain of personal development, remember that true progress emerges from a harmonious blend of introspection, action, and effective communication. By intertwining mindset, behavior, and communication through the lens of Extreme Dialogue, you're crafting a roadmap to tangible success. **Embrace this holistic perspective, and watch as your intentions transform into tangible outcomes, propelling you towards a future of fulfillment and achievement.**

CHAPTER 4: THE BLUEPRINT OF SUCCESS

Strategies that Drive Change

Transforming Words into Actionable Wins

The journey from dialogue to reality is paved with distinct strategies. Understanding and mastering these are pivotal for anyone seeking to translate ambitious dialogue into concrete success. This transformative path, delineated in the upcoming passages, is less about the grandeur of goals and more about the precision of the approach. Clarity of intention, mastery over language, adept use of visualization, meticulous action planning, and reflective practices are the keystones. Together, they create a foundation sturdy enough to not just withstand, but leverage the dynamic forces of change.

Clarity of intention is the initial lever. It's about piercing through the fog of ambiguity to pinpoint exactly what success looks like. This isn't merely wishful thinking; it's a deliberate process of aligning desires with tangible outcomes. By establishing clear intentions, individuals set the stage for a journey that's guided by purpose and precision. Moreover, **language mastery** is not just about eloquence but about employing language as a tool to shape reality. This involves framing aspirations in a manner that propels action and belief in one's ability to achieve set goals.

Visualization techniques serve as a catalyst in this mixture. They bridge the gap between abstract intentions and concrete reality. When individuals vividly imagine their success, they're not just dreaming; they're mentally rehearsing their triumphs. This mental rehearsal inscribes a blueprint of success into the subconscious, making the abstract tangibly imminent. Following closely, **action planning** transforms the vision into executable steps. It's about breaking down the journey into strategic milestones, creating a roadmap that's both ambitious and achievable.

However, the path from dialogue to reality is seldom straight. Here, **reflective practices** come into play. They act as a compass, guiding individuals through the unforeseen. By regularly evaluating progress and hurdles, individuals ensure that they stay on track or pivot efficiently when necessary. This continuous loop of action and reflection fosters a growth mindset, essential for navigating the complexities of turning dialogue into reality.

Crafting Success One Step at a Time

Step by Step: Crafting Clarity and Commanding Action

Reflect on Your Desires and Goals

Begin by investing time in introspection. Identify and document what you're genuinely aiming to achieve. Precision is key here; the clearer the goal, the more attainable it becomes.

Align Your Intentions with Your Values

The alignment between your intentions and your core values is crucial. This congruence ensures that your goals resonate deeply with who you are, amplifying both motivation and the sense of fulfillment from achieving them.

State Your Intentions in the Present Tense

Formulations in the present tense transform intentions from distant aspirations into current realities. This linguistic shift isn't merely semantic; it fundamentally alters your relationship with your goals, fostering a sense of immediacy and possibility.

Use Positive Language

The power of positive framing cannot be overstated. By articulating your intentions positively, you cultivate an environment ripe for growth and achievement. Negative language, conversely, can entrench limitations.

Make Your Intentions Specific and Measurable

General goals breed general results. Specificity, coupled with measurable criteria, brings discipline and focus, directing efforts more efficiently toward the desired outcomes.

Visualize Your Intentions

Immerse yourself in the successful achievement of your goals. This visualization is not idle dreaming but an active engagement with your success, enhancing motivation and the belief in its inevitability.

Write Down Your Intentions and Display Them

The physical act of writing and visibly displaying your intentions serves as a daily reminder of your commitments. It's a motivational tool that keeps the mind focused and aligned with your goals.

Review and Revisit Your Intentions Regularly

Consistent review and adjustment of your intentions ensure that you remain nimble, able to recalibrate your strategies in response to progress and challenges alike.

Take Action

Finally, transition from planning to execution. Break your intentions down into actionable steps and engage with them diligently. Success is less an event and more a process of consistent, directed action.

By navigating these steps with dedication and adaptability, individuals arm themselves with a structured approach to transforming dialogue into tangible achievements. This journey demands not just envisioning success but committing to the disciplined, reflective, and strategic pursuit of it.

Gain Clarity on Setting Intentions that Align with Desired Outcomes

Setting intentions is akin to planting seeds. Just as a farmer selects seeds based on the crop they wish to harvest, your intentions must be chosen with the desired outcomes clearly in mind. It's not enough to have a vague idea of wanting success or happiness. You need clarity, precision, and a deep understanding of what those terms mean to you personally. This clarity acts as a beacon, guiding your actions and decisions towards realizing your aspirations.

Consider for a moment a river flowing towards the ocean. It doesn't change its course haphazardly but follows a path carved by a combination of natural forces over time. Similarly, when your intentions are clear and aligned with your goals, your path to achieving them becomes more direct. You can navigate challenges more effectively because you know where you're headed and why. The force of your focused intention helps to overcome obstacles, much like water shapes its pathway through the landscape.

In a world brimming with distractions and alternative routes, maintaining focus on specified outcomes necessitates setting intentions with precision. Clear intentions serve as mental boundaries, helping to filter out distractions and center your energy on activities that propel you towards your goals. They are the measure against which every opportunity should be evaluated, ensuring each step taken is in the right direction.

Putting these concepts into practice involves introspection and honest appraisal of your desires and ambitions. It requires answering fundamental questions about what you truly want to achieve and why. This clarity doesn't come from a superficial glance at your aspirations but from a deep dive into your motivations and values. It's a process of aligning your heart, mind, and spirit with your goals, ensuring that the intentions set are genuinely reflective of your authentic self.

The key to unlocking tangible success lies in setting intentions with clarity and alignment to your desired outcomes.

The Art of Intention-Setting and Visualization Mastery

Reflect on Your Desires and Goals

The journey towards mastering language and visualization begins with introspection. Taking time to reflect on your desires and goals allows you a rare clarity that illuminates the path ahead. Like an artist facing a blank canvas, you hold the power to define the contours of your future with every stroke of intention.

Align Your Intentions with Your Values

Once the canvas of desire is set, aligning your intentions with your core values is equivalent to choosing the right colors for your masterpiece. This step ensures that every stroke resonates with the depth of your authentic self, making the outcome not just desirable but deeply fulfilling.

State Your Intentions in the Present Tense

Articulating intentions in the present tense is akin to painting with bold and vibrant colors. It breathes life into your aspirations, making them more tangible and immediate. This practice fosters a mindset of abundance and attainment, vital for nurturing belief in the fruition of your intents.

Use Positive Language

Positive language serves as the light that illuminates your masterpiece, highlighting possibilities and radiating warmth. It creates an inviting aura around your intentions, attracting the energies and opportunities compatible with your aspirations.

Make Your Intentions Specific and Measurable

Detailing your intentions with specificity is like adding intricate details to your painting. It brings clarity and focus, enabling you to direct your efforts more efficiently and measure progress accurately.

Visualize Your Intentions

Visualization is the act of imbuing your canvas with emotion and sensation, making your vision vividly alive. It's a powerful technique that bridges the gap between intention and reality, anchoring your desires in the subconscious.

Write Down Your Intentions and Display Them

Writing down your intentions and displaying them is akin to signing your name on your completed masterpiece. It's a declaration of ownership and a constant reminder of your commitment to bringing your vision to life.

Review and Revisit Your Intentions Regularly

Regularly reviewing your intentions is like stepping back to evaluate your painting. It allows you to appreciate your progress, make necessary adjustments, and renew your commitment to the creative process.

Take Action

Finally, taking action is the act of applying brush to canvas, transforming vision into reality. Each stroke is a step towards manifesting your intentions, guided by the plan you've meticulously crafted through this process.

Could reframing our intentions and visualizations in the present tense be the key to unlocking their full potential?

The Success Alignment Model (SAM)

The Success Alignment Model (SAM) is designed to transform intentions into tangible outcomes through a cyclical process of Define, Align, Act, and Reflect.

Define

In the Define phase, one sets the stage by specifying goals with precision. This act mirrors an artist selecting a theme for their work—setting a clear and focused direction that guides all subsequent actions. Precision in defining your goals clarifies what success looks like and establishes a firm foundation for the journey ahead.

Align

Alignment ensures that the chosen path resonates deeply with one's core values and beliefs, integrating the insights from cognitive behavioral therapy with the principles of Extreme Dialogue. This phase is crucial for sustainability and authenticity, ensuring that the journey towards achieving set goals is as enriching as the destination itself.

Act

Taking action is about applying the techniques of language mastery and visualization to move towards defined goals. Actions are deliberate, purposeful, and informed by the clarity gained in the previous phases. This stage brings the vision into reality, one step at a time, leveraging the power of intentional language and vivid imagery to maintain momentum.

Reflect

Reflection allows for evaluation and continuous improvement. It's a time to assess the effectiveness of actions taken, learn from the outcomes, and make necessary adjustments. This phase emphasizes growth and adaptability, fostering resilience and the agility to pivot strategies as needed to stay aligned with evolving goals.

Through this cyclical process, the Success Alignment Model (SAM) facilitates a dynamic approach to achieving goals. It's a model that recognizes the fluid nature of aspirations and the necessity of continuous alignment with personal growth and change.

By embracing the cyclical nature of defining, aligning, acting, and reflecting, individuals can navigate their journey to success with greater clarity, purpose, and flexibility.

Reflecting on Success Strategies

In mastering the strategies outlined in this chapter, one thing becomes abundantly clear: **success is not a matter of mere chance**; it is a result of deliberate actions and focused intentions. By honing your skills in setting clear intentions, mastering your language, harnessing visualization techniques, creating actionable plans, and engaging in reflective practices, you are **equipped to navigate the path from dialogue to tangible wins**.

Moving Forward with Purpose

With clarity of intention, you pave the way for your desired outcomes. Through language mastery and visualization techniques, you amplify your aspirations into reality. Action plans ensure progress, while reflection allows for refinement and growth. **This blueprint of success is your roadmap to achievement.**

The Power of Implementation

Putting these strategies into action is where the real magic happens. Your intentions become tangible, your words carry weight, and your plans unfold into results. **Every step you take, fueled by these strategies, brings you closer to your goals**. Keep moving forward with purpose and unwavering determination.

Embracing Change through Action

Success is not a destination; it is a journey of continuous improvement. By implementing the strategies discussed, you embrace change as an opportunity for growth. Each adjustment, each pivot, is a step towards evolution and success. **Embrace change, take action, and watch your dreams materialize**.

In the realm of Extreme Dialogue, your success is not just a possibility; it is a certainty when armed with the right strategies and mindset. As you apply these principles in your daily pursuits, remember that each intentional step forward is a step closer to realizing your true potential. Through mastery of intention, language, visualization, action, and reflection, you are not just shaping your future; you are sculpting a legacy of triumph and fulfillment.

CHAPTER 5: REINVENTING SELF-IMPROVEMENT

The Evolution with Extreme Dialogue

> *What revelations might reveal themselves if we allowed the seeds of Extreme Dialogue to take root within the soil of our being?*

Transform Your Self-Improvement Journey with Extreme Dialogue

Extreme Dialogue is more than just a new buzzword in the realm of personal development; it is a revolutionary approach that challenges and transforms the traditional paths of self-improvement. This methodology leverages the power of intentional thought and focused conversation to unlock a level of personal growth and professional success previously untapped by conventional strategies. By deeply analyzing the transformative impact of Extreme Dialogue on personal growth, individuals can begin to navigate their self-improvement journeys with more precision and intention.

One of the first steps in embracing Extreme Dialogue is recognizing the need for a shift in perspective when it comes to enhancing traditional personal development strategies. Traditional methods often focus on singular goals and linear progression, overlooking the dynamic nature of personal growth. Extreme Dialogue, on the other hand, encourages an iterative process of reflection, learning, and adaptation. This approach not only cultivates a growth mindset but also builds resilience in the face of challenges, enabling individuals to pursue their goals with greater agility and confidence.

The implementation of Extreme Dialogue necessitates a deep understanding of one's intentions and the language used to express them. It's about forging a connection between thought, language, and action that is so strong, it propels individuals towards their desired outcomes with an unprecedented focus and clarity. The *discipline of articulating one's thoughts and desires* explicitly can significantly enhance decision-making and goal-setting processes, making them more aligned with one's core values and aspirations.

Moreover, the strategic application of Extreme Dialogue extends beyond individual growth; it has profound implications for professional endeavors as well. In today's fast-paced, ever-evolving business landscape, the ability to communicate effectively and create meaningful connections is invaluable. Extreme Dialogue fosters authentic communication, promoting transparency, and trust, which are essential for building strong professional relationships and collaborative teams. It supports a culture of continuous learning and innovation, encouraging individuals and organizations to think outside the box and pursue creative solutions to complex challenges.

Analytics and metrics play a crucial role in measuring the impact of Extreme Dialogue on personal and professional growth. By setting clear benchmarks and regularly evaluating progress, individuals and teams can gain insights into the effectiveness of their efforts and iterate their strategies for better results. This data-driven approach ensures that the application of Extreme Dialogue is grounded in tangible outcomes, making the path to success more visible and attainable.

Achieving Tangible Success with Intentional Conversations

The journey of self-improvement with Extreme Dialogue is both a personal and collective endeavor. It requires individuals to be deeply introspective while also being open to feedback and collaboration. This balanced approach enables people to not only enhance their own growth but also contribute to the growth of others around them. By prioritizing genuine connections and fostering a supportive community, the philosophy of Extreme Dialogue cultivates an environment where collective success is celebrated as much as individual achievements.

In essence, Extreme Dialogue is a tool that transforms the landscape of personal development and professional growth. By understanding its transformative power, recognizing the need for a perspective shift, and evaluating its broader implications, individuals and organizations alike can harness the full potential of intentional thought and language. This method not only paves the way for achieving personal and professional goals but also redefines the very notion of success, making it more meaningful and fulfilling.

Extreme Dialogue has been positioned as a groundbreaking method in the landscape of personal growth. At its core, it leverages intentional conversation as a tool not only for self-improvement but as a vehicle for profound personal transformation. The dynamic nature of Extreme Dialogue encourages individuals to delve deeper into their thought processes, motivations, and, ultimately, the articulation of their personal and professional aspirations. This method fosters an environment where growth is not just a byproduct but a deliberate outcome of structured, meaningful engagement with oneself and others.

Imagine a garden where each conversation is like watering a specific plant. Just as water prompts plants to grow, nourish, and bloom, Extreme Dialogue stimulates personal growth in a similarly organic but intentional manner. This analogy underscores the transformative potential of Extreme Dialogue when applied to personal development. It's not about the volume of water but the frequency and the mindful targeting of it that brings about the most vibrant blooms. In this light, personal growth, akin to gardening, becomes a series of intentional actions rather than random occurrences.

The methodology behind Extreme Dialogue is designed to challenge and dismantle the barriers that often hinder personal development. It addresses the fundamental need for vulnerability and courage in conversations about personal aspirations, failures, and successes. By fostering a culture of openness and authenticity, Extreme Dialogue facilitates a level of introspection and self-awareness that traditional personal development methods often overlook. This emphasis on genuine engagement helps individuals to identify and align their values with their actions, leading to more meaningful and sustained personal growth.

Statistics and testimonials have repeatedly underscored the effectiveness of integrating dialogue-based approaches into personal development plans. Participants report increased clarity in their goals, improved relationships, and a stronger sense of self-worth. This quantitative and qualitative feedback highlights the profound impact that structured dialogue can have on an individual's growth trajectory.

The transformative impact of Extreme Dialogue on personal growth lies in its ability to foster deeper understanding, intentional action, and sustained self-improvement.

Recognize the Shift in Perspective Needed to Enhance Traditional Personal Development Strategies

Traditional personal development strategies often emphasize goal setting, habit formation, and self-discipline. While these elements are crucial, they sometimes leave little room for the exploration of the deeper psychological and emotional facets of self-improvement. Extreme Dialogue introduces a paradigm shift, suggesting that the bedrock of personal development lies not just in what we do but in how we communicate with ourselves and others about our aspirations and challenges.

The power of perspective in personal development cannot be overstated. A shift in how we view our goals and challenges can dramatically alter our approach to overcoming them. Think of it as wearing a new pair of glasses; suddenly, what was blurry becomes clear. Extreme Dialogue encourages us to 'change our glasses,' so to speak, to view our goals and obstacles through a lens of compassion, curiosity, and open-mindedness. This perspective shift is pivotal in transforming obstacles into opportunities for growth.

Rhetorically speaking, how often do we truly listen to understand, rather than to respond? Extreme Dialogue champions the art of active listening and mindful response, which are essential for meaningful personal journeys. These skills enable individuals to process information more deeply, challenge their preconceptions, and embrace new ideas and perspectives. This approach not only enriches personal development but also enhances communication skills, leading to more constructive interactions in all areas of life.

One analogy to consider is that of Extreme Dialogue being akin to a sculptor shaping clay. In this process, the sculptor must be both deliberate and open to the evolving form of the sculpture. Similarly, individuals engaging in Extreme Dialogue must remain flexible and responsive to their changing thoughts, emotions, and circumstances, all while maintaining a clear vision of their personal development goals. This dynamic process of shaping and reshaping one's self-concept is at the heart of enhanced personal development strategies.

To put it succinctly, Extreme Dialogue necessitates a willingness to venture into uncharted territories of self-exploration and communication. This journey is not without its challenges, but the rewards – deeper self-understanding, improved relationships, and enhanced personal fulfillment – are well worth the effort.

Could it be that the key to unlocking our full potential lies not in more rigorous planning and execution, but in transforming the way we communicate with ourselves and the world around us?

Evaluate the Broader Implications of Applying Intentional Thought and Language in Professional Endeavors

Intentional thought and language, the pillars of Extreme Dialogue, are not confined to personal growth alone; they have profound implications in the professional sphere as well. Businesses and organizations stand to gain significantly from adopting these principles. Communication strategies informed by intentionality foster clearer objectives, more efficient problem-solving, and bolstered team dynamics. This approach directly translates to increased productivity, enhanced innovation, and a stronger organizational culture.

Consider the metaphor of a boat sailing towards a destination. Intentional thought and language serve as both the compass and the rudder, guiding the vessel through calm and turbulent waters alike. Just as the captain must adjust the sails and rudder with purpose and precision to reach their destination, leaders must navigate their teams through challenges and opportunities with clear, purposeful communication. This analogy underscores the pivotal role that intentionality plays in steering professional endeavors towards success.

The implementation of Extreme Dialogue in a professional context encourages a culture of open communication and collaborative problem-solving. By promoting an environment where employees feel valued and heard, organizations can unlock a higher level of creativity and engagement among their team members. This not only boosts morale but also leads to more innovative solutions to business challenges.

Data from various industries highlights the impact of adopting intentional communication strategies on employee satisfaction and retention rates. Organizations that prioritize meaningful dialogue report a marked improvement in team cohesion and a decrease in conflict, underscoring the tangible benefits of integrating Extreme Dialogue into professional practices.

The broader implications of applying intentional thought and language extend far beyond personal development, promising to revolutionize professional relationships and organizational effectiveness. The principles of Extreme Dialogue, when embraced fully, elevate both individual and collective endeavors, bridging the gap between intention and realization.

Extreme Dialogue has proven to be a transformative force in the realm of personal growth, offering a fresh perspective that challenges the status quo of traditional self-improvement methodologies. Through intentional thought and language, individuals have unlocked the power to shape their realities and manifest their deepest desires. **The shift in perspective brought about by Extreme Dialogue has illuminated new pathways for growth and success, pushing individuals to think beyond limitations and embrace the boundless potential within themselves.**

By actively engaging in intentional conversations with oneself and others, individuals can redefine their approach to personal development and professional endeavors. This evolution marks a turning point in understanding the profound impact of language and thought on shaping our reality. The intentional use of words can catalyze transformation and empower individuals to navigate challenges with confidence and clarity.

As we delve deeper into the broader implications of intentional thought and language in professional settings, it becomes evident that **the fusion of Extreme Dialogue with professional endeavors can lead to unparalleled success.** By harnessing the power of intentional communication, individuals can build authentic connections, foster trust, and drive meaningful collaborations. This strategic approach not only enhances productivity and innovation but also cultivates a culture of transparency and shared vision within teams.

As we look towards the future, it is imperative to embrace the evolution that Extreme Dialogue offers in personal and professional growth. By honing the art of intentional thought and language, individuals can unlock their true potential, transform their realities, and pave the way for extraordinary achievements. Let us continue to harness the power of words and thoughts to propel ourselves towards tangible success and fulfillment.

CHAPTER 6: UNLEASHING POTENTIAL

Young Professionals and Entrepreneurs

> *What changes might unfold if young professionals and entrepreneurs embraced not just the technology and data analysis, but the transformative power of dialogue? Could it be the key to not just surviving but thriving in this complex business world?*

Unlocking the Power of Extreme Dialogue for the Next Generation

In today's fast-paced world, young professionals and entrepreneurs stand at the forefront of innovation and progress, always on the hunt for strategies that not only enhance personal development but also ensure productivity is at its peak. The search for such methods has led to the emergence of Extreme Dialogue as a preferred approach. This method is not merely about communication; it's about transforming dialogue into definitive action and tangible results. The unique requirements of this demographic, coupled with their inclination towards pioneering solutions, make them an ideal audience for the Extreme Dialogue methodology.

Young professionals and entrepreneurs possess a distinct set of needs when it comes to personal development. They are not content with traditional methods that offer generic advice without actionable outcomes. What they seek are performance-based solutions that can be measured and optimized. **Extreme Dialogue** caters precisely to this need, offering an actionable approach to personal growth. By focusing on results and data analysis, this method appeals to the rational mind while encouraging a culture of innovation and creativity.

The appeal of innovative methods like Extreme Dialogue to this demographic is palpable. In an era dominated by technology and data analysis, young professionals and entrepreneurs are drawn to methodologies that synthesize these elements with personal growth. The inclination towards such innovative solutions stems from their desire to bridge the gap between the digital and personal domains. Extreme Dialogue, with its emphasis on measurable outcomes and actionable insights, resonates deeply with their professional ethos.

Practical outcomes from mindset shifts form the cornerstone of Extreme Dialogue's appeal. For young professionals and entrepreneurs, the transition from traditional thought processes to those that are more dynamic and results-oriented is crucial. The methodology promotes not just a shift in thinking but in achieving observable, tangible outcomes. This shift is facilitated by focusing on **growth hacking techniques**, marketing strategies, and content creation, all tailored to suit their specific professional contexts. It's about transforming words into wins, mastering the art of manifestation with precision rather than leaving it to guesswork.

Collaboration and teamwork are emphasized, underscoring the significance of forming genuine relationships based on trust and transparency. The methodology does not operate in isolation but encourages networking and partnerships that can amplify results. In doing so, Extreme Dialogue fosters an environment where young professionals and entrepreneurs can thrive, fueled by mutual respect and shared objectives.

Innovation and creativity are at the heart of Extreme Dialogue.

By encouraging individuals to think outside the box and exhibit intellectual curiosity, the methodology ensures that young professionals and entrepreneurs are not just participants in their respective fields but pioneers. The focus on authentic connections and transparent communication further enriches this experience, making the journey towards personal and professional development as rewarding as the destination.

Extreme Dialogue is not just a method; it's a movement. It inspires young professionals and entrepreneurs to transcend traditional boundaries, empowering them to unlock their full potential. By identifying their unique needs, understanding the appeal of innovative methods, and discovering practical outcomes from mindset shifts, individuals are equipped to navigate the complexities of their professional endeavors with confidence and clarity. The result is a generation of leaders who are not just prepared for the future but are actively shaping it.

Identifying the Unique Needs of Young Professionals and Entrepreneurs

Young professionals and entrepreneurs are continually searching for avenues to distinct themselves in a competitive market. The quest for personal development among them is not just about accumulating knowledge but about finding innovative strategies to enhance productivity, leadership, and personal growth. This demographic's unique set of professional aspirations and lifestyle pressures necessitates a tailored approach to personal development, diverging from traditional, one-size-fits-all solutions.

Imagine personal development as a meticulously tailored suit. For young professionals and entrepreneurs, off-the-rack solutions simply won't suffice. They require a bespoke fit — strategies and insights directly applicable to the fast-paced world they navigate. This tailored approach ensures that personal development strategies are directly relevant to their unique challenges and goals, increasing the likelihood of significant personal and professional progression.

The digital age has also transformed the expectations and learning styles of young professionals and entrepreneurs. Accustomed to the instantaneity of information and communication technologies, this demographic seeks personal development resources that are not only effective but also accessible and concise. They value practicality over theory, action over contemplation, looking for methods that deliver noticeable results without detracting from their time-sensitive endeavors.

The realms of teamwork, leadership, and emotional intelligence are particular areas of focus for young professionals and entrepreneurs in their personal development journey. This focus is not just about climbing the corporate ladder but about fostering meaningful relationships, inspiring their teams, and leading with empathy and inclusivity. They are in pursuit of personal growth that is not only beneficial to their career but also enriches their personal life and well-being.

In essence, the unique needs of young professionals and entrepreneurs in personal development revolve around tailor-made, practical, and time-efficient strategies that balance professional aspirations with personal well-being.

Why Extreme Dialogue Appeals to Young Professionals and Entrepreneurs

The innovative approach of Extreme Dialogue aligns perfectly with the ambitions of young professionals and entrepreneurs. It introduces a fresh perspective on personal development, prioritizing actionable steps and mindset shifts over traditional didactic learning methods. So, why does this methodology resonate so strongly with this demographic?

For starters, Extreme Dialogue thrives on engagement

and interaction, mirroring the dynamic environments these individuals operate in. It's like swapping a lecture for a workshop where participants are not just passive listeners but active contributors. This interactive model fosters a deeper understanding and application of personal development concepts, ensuring that the learning experience is both engaging and effective.

Moreover, Extreme Dialogue champions the concept of learning by doing. It's akin to a chef honing their skills not by reading recipe books but by cooking, tasting, and adjusting. In the same vein, young professionals and entrepreneurs appreciate this hands-on approach, as it mirrors the reality of the business world where theoretical knowledge must be applied and tested in real scenarios.

The methodology also offers a degree of flexibility and adaptability that is highly valued by this demographic. In the fast-changing landscapes of technology and business, strategies and solutions that can evolve and pivot are paramount. Extreme Dialogue's emphasis on continual learning and adaptability resembles a tech startup's agile development process, resonating with the entrepreneurial mindset that values iteration and innovation.

Why does the dialogue-driven, action-oriented approach of Extreme Dialogue specifically appeal to the entrepreneurial spirit and the innovative minds of young professionals?

Practical Outcomes from Mindset Shifts

The crux of Extreme Dialogue lies in fostering mindset shifts that lead to tangible outcomes. For young professionals and entrepreneurs, these shifts are not abstract transformations but practical changes with visible impacts on their professional and personal lives.

Imagine planting a garden where the mindset shift is akin to preparing the soil. It's a foundational step, invisible to onlookers, yet it determines the health and growth of everything that sprouts. Similarly, adopting a growth mindset, embracing failure as a stepping stone, and seeing challenges as opportunities can transform the landscape of a young professional's career, leading to innovation, resilience, and, ultimately, success.

One practical outcome of embracing the principles of Extreme Dialogue is enhanced decision-making. In a world where young entrepreneurs constantly navigate uncertainty, the ability to make informed, timely decisions is invaluable. This boon stems from the shift towards a more open, analytical, and reflective mindset, empowering them to weigh options more effectively and foresee the impact of their choices.

Another tangible benefit is improved communication. In the collaborative environments that dominate the modern workplace, the ability to articulate ideas clearly, listen actively, and empathize with others' perspectives is paramount. Through the practice of Extreme Dialogue, participants learn to value diverse viewpoints, reducing conflicts and fostering a culture of innovation driven by shared goals.

Increased resilience is also a notable outcome. The entrepreneurial journey is fraught with challenges and setbacks. A shifted mindset, however, equips young professionals with the mental fortitude to persevere, viewing each obstacle as a learning opportunity rather than a defeat.

By intertwining the exploration of mindset shifts with practical, real-world applications, Extreme Dialogue promises young professionals and entrepreneurs not just personal growth but tangible, observable improvements in their professional endeavors and personal lives.

In the realm of personal development, young professionals and entrepreneurs stand at the forefront, eager to evolve, adapt, and excel. This dynamic demographic craves practical methods that yield tangible outcomes, embracing innovative approaches that promise not just growth but concrete results. The appeal of Extreme Dialogue lies in its ability to bridge the gap between cutting-edge technology, data analysis, and personal advancement. With a keen eye on productivity and self-improvement, this audience finds solace in strategies that go beyond theoretical wisdom and dive deep into actionable steps that drive real change.

The journey towards unlocking potential in young professionals and entrepreneurs is paved with a blend of innovation and practicality, where mindset shifts serve as the fuel for transformation. By recognizing the unique needs of this demographic, we pave the way for growth hacking strategies that catalyze progress and enhance performance. Understanding their thirst for new ideas and approaches, Extreme Dialogue emerges as a beacon of hope, offering a pathway to success that resonates with their tech-savvy, data-driven mindset.

As young professionals and entrepreneurs immerse themselves in the world of Extreme Dialogue, they are poised to witness a cascade of practical outcomes stemming from refined mindsets and strategic shifts. Embracing this methodology unlocks a realm of possibilities, propelling individuals towards achievements that were once confined to dreams. Through the fusion of cutting-edge techniques and personal development, this audience is empowered to soar to new heights, armed with the tools to conquer challenges head-on and emerge victorious in the competitive landscape of modern business and personal growth.

CHAPTER 7: NEW HORIZONS IN 'SELF-HELP'

A Fresh Perspective

> *If action, pure and unbridled, could flow from through you without the paralysis of overthought. What steps would you take to turn your intentions into undeniable action?*

Transcending Traditional Boundaries

The landscape of self-help and personal development is continuously evolving, with enthusiasts constantly seeking innovative approaches to enrich their personal growth journey. One such groundbreaking methodology is Extreme Dialogue—a technique designed to transform abstract mindset concepts into tangible realities. This shift towards a more concrete and measurable approach in personal development is both refreshing and necessary for those looking to make significant strides in their lives.

Extreme Dialogue stands out as a powerful tool in the realm of self-improvement, fundamentally altering how individuals perceive and interact with their goals. By fostering a deeper understanding of the dialogue we engage in with ourselves, it enables us to translate our thoughts and intentions into actionable outcomes. This method is not about mere wishful thinking; it's about creating a structured pathway from ideation to realization, distinguishing itself from traditional self-help methods that often remain trapped in the realm of theory.

For personal development enthusiasts, the allure of a fresh perspective cannot be overstated. The thirst for innovative strategies that break away from conventional wisdom is omnipresent. **Extreme Dialogue offers this breath of fresh air**, providing a unique lens through which to view personal growth. It does not merely suggest that change is possible; it outlines a clear and practical roadmap to achieve it. This appeals to individuals looking for more than inspiration—they seek transformation.

Bridging the Gap between Theory and Practice

Discovering actionable approaches for implementing self-improvement theories in real life is a significant challenge for many. Extreme Dialogue addresses this head-on by demystifying the process of manifesting thoughts into reality. It emphasizes the importance of clear, focused communication with oneself, setting the stage for meaningful personal progress. By teaching users to refine their internal dialogues, it equips them with the skills needed to effectively translate abstract concepts into concrete actions.

Moreover, Extreme Dialogue underscores the critical role of metrics, analytics, and data analysis in tracking personal growth. This resonates with professionals accustomed to employing these tools in growth hacking, marketing strategy, and content creation. Just as these disciplines rely on measurable outcomes to gauge success, Extreme Dialogue introduces similar metrics to the self-help domain, allowing individuals to monitor their progress and adjust their strategies accordingly.

Fostering Genuine Connections and Creativity

At its core, Extreme Dialogue encourages the formation of genuine relationships with oneself and others. It promotes trust, transparency, and authenticity—qualities essential for any successful personal development endeavor. By prioritizing these values, individuals can embark on their growth journeys with confidence and clarity, knowing they are building on a solid foundation of self-awareness and genuine intent.

Furthermore, Extreme Dialogue sparks creativity and innovation, urging individuals to think outside the box and explore new possibilities. It challenges users to question established norms and to envision alternative pathways to their goals. This emphasis on intellectual curiosity drives personal exploration to new depths, ensuring that growth is not only attainable but also sustainable and fulfilling.

Conclusion

Extreme Dialogue is more than just another self-help technique—it's a paradigm shift in how we approach personal development. By offering fresh perspectives, actionable strategies, and a focus on tangible outcomes, it empowers individuals to transform their lives in profound ways. For those dedicated to their growth journey, embracing Extreme Dialogue could indeed be the key to unlocking a new horizon of possibilities.

Recognizing the Thirst for Fresh Takes Among Personal Development Enthusiasts

In the realm of self-help and personal development, enthusiasts are continually on the lookout for new perspectives and methods that promise not just inspiration but real transformation. This pursuit is driven by a deep-seated desire for growth and self-improvement. Just as a gardener seeks new cultivation techniques to enrich their soil and yield better crops, individuals dedicated to self-improvement seek novel approaches that promise to enrich their lives.

One could liken the search for fresh takes in the personal development field to explorers seeking new territories. These explorers aren't satisfied with treading the same path repeatedly;

they crave undiscovered lands and the promise of new horizons. Similarly, individuals engaged in personal growth are always on the lookout for innovative ideas and strategies that deviate from the well-trodden path. This incessant pursuit stems from the belief that there is always a better, more effective way to achieve personal growth.

The landscape of personal development is vast, and the thirst for new perspectives is partly a response to the dynamic nature of human beings. What works for one individual may not resonate with another, making the quest for versatile and innovative self-help methodologies ever more critical. Additionally, as our understanding of the human mind and behavior evolves, so too do the strategies for personal improvement. This evolution encourages a continuous search for updated and comprehensive approaches that align with the latest psychological insights.

Extreme Dialogue stands out in this context, offering a pathway that diverges from traditional self-improvement methods. By fostering a deep and meaningful conversation with oneself and transforming these dialogues into concrete actions, this approach presents a refreshing and practical way of bridging the gap between aspiration and reality.

Key point: Recognize the perpetual quest of personal development enthusiasts for innovative and effective methods to catalyze their growth.

How Extreme Dialogue Offers a Novel Way to Manifest Thoughts into Reality

In the scenic landscape of self-help methodologies, Extreme Dialogue emerges as a distinctive path cutting through the familiar terrain. At its core, Extreme Dialogue is not merely about positive thinking or visualizing success; it's about deeply engaging with one's thoughts and ideas to manifest tangible outcomes. This process resembles not just planting seeds with expectation but conversing with them, understanding their needs, and nurturing them to fruition.

What sets Extreme Dialogue apart is its emphasis on action. It acknowledges that thoughts are the blueprint for our realities, yet without action, they are as ephemeral as clouds. Just as an architect draws up detailed plans for a structure but must then take the concrete steps to build it, Extreme Dialogue encourages individuals to move beyond dreaming into doing.

Imagine, for a moment, a bridge. On one side, you have your wealth of thoughts, ideas, and aspirations. On the opposite bank lies the reality of your desires manifested. Extreme Dialogue serves as the structure that connects these two worlds. It's about crafting a dialogue so profound with oneself that it propels action, bridging the divide between thought and actualization.

Many self-help methodologies focus on the power of thought alone, underscoring the importance of maintaining a positive mindset. While undeniably important, Extreme Dialogue advances this concept by insisting on the critical role of conversation—both internal and external—as a catalyst for change. Through thoughtfully structured dialogues, it invites participants to dissect, challenge, and reframe their perspectives, leading to a deliberate and actionable plan for personal development.

The simplicity of this approach belies its transformative potential. By fostering a deep and dynamic engagement with one's thoughts and ideas, Extreme Dialogue facilitates a process where abstract aspirations are distilled into clear, achievable goals. This method demonstrates that the act of profound self-conversation can be the most powerful tool in turning dreams into reality.

Could the key to unlocking your potential lie in the art of conversation with oneself?

Discover Actionable Approaches for Bridging

Theory and Practice in Self-Improvement

The journey from theoretical knowledge to practical application in self-improvement is akin to crossing a vast river. On one bank lies the theoretical knowledge—rich, diverse, and full of potential. Across the river awaits the practical application—the realization of this knowledge in tangible results. The challenge, however, lies in building the bridge that connects these two banks. This is where the actionable approaches of Extreme Dialogue come into play, serving as the foundation and structure for this crucial bridge.

Just as a bridge requires a detailed blueprint, clear materials, and a step-by-step building process, applying theories of self-improvement to real-life scenarios necessitates a structured approach. Extreme Dialogue offers precisely this: a concrete framework for taking the abstract concepts of self-help and personal development and translating them into actionable steps. This method is centered around the power of internal dialogue, turning introspective conversation into a tool for tangible change.

One of the cornerstone principles of Extreme Dialogue is the belief that self-conversation can systematically break down larger goals into manageable actions. Much like how a sculptor sees a remarkable figure within a block of marble and chisels away bit by bit to reveal it, Extreme Dialogue teaches individuals to parse their aspirations into clear, achievable tasks. This process not only makes daunting goals more attainable but also demystifies the journey from theory to practice.

By emphasizing clarity, focus, and action, Extreme Dialogue demarcates a clear path forward. It understands that while inspiration and motivation are crucial, they must be paired with actionable steps that individuals can take to make their dreams a reality. Through this method, the gap between wanting and achieving is bridged, turning the theoretical into the practical.

Extreme Dialogue emerges as a comprehensive approach, **blending the power of internal dialogue with actionable steps** **to manifest thoughts into reality and bridge the gap between** **theory and practice in self-improvement.**

In the realm of self-help and personal development, the hunger for innovation is insatiable. Those committed to their growth journey are constantly seeking fresh perspectives to invigorate their mindset and spur tangible progress. *Extreme Dialogue serves as a beacon of originality,* offering a groundbreaking method to turn aspirations into concrete realities. **By embracing this novel approach, individuals can transform abstract theories into** *actionable steps*, **forging a seamless link between conceptual frameworks and practical implementation.**

The landscape of personal growth is shifting towards a more hands-on, results-driven approach. *Embracing the principles of Extreme Dialogue equips individuals with the tools* to navigate this evolving terrain with confidence and clarity. **Through a blend of theory and practice, personal development enthusiasts can transcend mere contemplation and take bold steps towards their aspirations.** *By adopting actionable strategies and fostering a mindset primed for success, individuals can navigate the waters of self-improvement with resilience and purpose.*

As you embark on your journey towards personal growth and transformation, remember the significance of fresh perspectives and innovative tools like Extreme Dialogue. *Incorporate these novel strategies into your daily routine*, bridging the gap between theory and practice in self-improvement. **By infusing your mindset with a spirit of innovation and a commitment to tangible results, you pave the way for profound change and unwavering progress.**

CHAPTER 8: AMPLIFYING IMPACT

Educators and Coaches

> *In the quietude of sanctuary, with the echoes of countless conversations, I wondered, did the key to unlocking the finest potential of human development lie in the courage to embrace the intensity of crucial conversations?*

Unlock the Power of Extreme Dialogue in Personal Development

The role of educators and coaches in the personal development sector cannot be overstated—these professionals possess the unique ability to guide individuals towards achieving their fullest potential. In an era where personal growth is highly sought after, applying **Extreme Dialogue principles** to personal development practices promises to revolutionize the way educators and coaches operate. This approach isn't just a method; it's a transformative experience that empowers professionals to deepen their impact and enrich their guidance processes. By uncovering the essence of Extreme Dialogue, educators and coaches can elevate their ability to foster meaningful progress in others' lives.

At the heart of Extreme Dialogue lies the capacity to **engage deeply with one's thoughts and emotions**, encouraging an authentic exploration of self. For professionals in the personal development field, integrating these principles means adopting a new paradigm—one that champions open-mindedness, continuous learning, and genuine connection. This chapter delves into how this innovative approach can not only amplify the personal growth of practitioners themselves but also significantly enhance the way they mentor and support others. The application of Extreme Dialogue extends far beyond traditional talking therapies or coaching methods; it's about instilling a mindset that embraces challenges as opportunities for growth.

Understanding the **multiplier effect** of these principles when applied to coaching and education is crucial. As educators and coaches incorporate Extreme Dialogue into their practices, they catalyze a ripple effect, empowering countless individuals to embark on their self-improvement journeys with renewed confidence and clarity. This isn't just about improving individual sessions or interactions; it's about fostering an environment where open dialogue, critical thinking, and personal introspection flourish.

Moreover, mastering strategies for advising others on their self-improvement journeys is paramount. Extreme Dialogue encourages a shift away from prescriptive advice, instead advocating for a co-creative process where the coach or educator and the individual work in tandem. This collaborative approach paves the way for solutions that are not only highly personalized but also deeply resonant with the individual's unique experiences and aspirations.

Through **practical insights and real-world examples**, this chapter will offer a comprehensive guide on how to seamlessly integrate Extreme Dialogue into personal development practices. Readers will gain actionable strategies to enhance their coaching techniques, making them more effective and impactful. By focusing on building genuine relationships, fostering transparency, and encouraging innovation, educators and coaches can unlock new dimensions of success for those they assist.

Above all, embracing Extreme Dialogue is about more than just enhancing professional practices; it's a journey towards genuine self-improvement and personal evolution. As educators and coaches embody the principles of Extreme Dialogue, they not only transform the lives of those they guide but also experience profound personal growth. This dual pathway to development strengthens the personal development sector as a whole, setting a new standard for how growth is facilitated and achieved.

Empowering others to transform their dialogue into tangible success is the ultimate goal. By guiding individuals through the nuanced process of translating their words into actions, educators and coaches play a pivotal role in unlocking their potential. As this chapter unfolds, it will illuminate how applying Extreme Dialogue can significantly amplify the impact of personal development professionals, ultimately leading to transformative changes that echo across all aspects of life.

Extreme Dialogue principles stand at the confluence of communication, empathy, and deep understanding, offering a powerful suite of tools for personal development. By weaving these principles into the fabric of personal development practices, educators and coaches can unlock new levels of growth, both for themselves and those they guide. This fusion instills a profound sense of awareness and connection, fostering environments where transformative conversations become the catalyst for personal evolution.

Within the realm of personal development, the journey toward self-improvement often mirrors the ascent of a climber tackling a formidable mountain. Each handhold represents a new skill or insight gained, each ledge a milestone reached. Applying Extreme Dialogue principles is akin to equipping climbers with the best gear and a seasoned guide. It's about enhancing the clarity of the path ahead and ensuring the journey is as enriching as reaching the summit. This analogy underscores the substantial impact these principles can have when integrated into personal development frameworks.

Educators and coaches have always played a pivotal role in guiding individuals through the intricate landscape of personal growth. With the addition of Extreme Dialogue principles, they possess an augmented toolkit that enables them to delve deeper into the psyches of those they assist, fostering an environment ripe for profound growth and self-discovery. These tools emphasize the importance of authentic communication, active listening, and the nurturing of empathy, thereby enhancing the effectiveness of personal development practices.

When applied judiciously, Extreme Dialogue principles magnify the transformative power of personal development interventions. By focusing on enriching the communicative bridges between educator and learner, these methodologies facilitate breakthroughs that might otherwise remain elusive. The essence of this approach is not just in teaching or coaching but in igniting a journey of discovery that is both shared and deeply personal.

The key point is that integrating Extreme Dialogue principles significantly elevates personal development practices by enhancing communicative efficiency and empathy.

Understand the Multiplier Effect

The impact of integrating Extreme Dialogue principles into coaching and education transcends the immediate interactions. It initiates a ripple effect, wherein each individual touched by these enriched methodologies carries forward the essence of the teachings, seeding transformative dialogues in their own circles. Think of it as lighting a beacon that guides not just a single ship to shore but an entire fleet. This multiplier effect embodies the expansive potential of these principles to foster understanding and growth beyond the initial point of contact.

Integrating Extreme Dialogue into coaching or educational frameworks fundamentally alters the landscape of personal interaction. It's akin to upgrading from a two-dimensional map to a three-dimensional one, offering richer, more nuanced guidance. This upgrade not only benefits the direct recipients but also equips them to engage more effectively with others, magnifying the impact through each conversation they subsequently navigate.

Rhetorically, one might ask how such a profound multiplier effect can be quantified. The answer lies in observing the shifts in personal and professional environments where these principles have been applied. Increased empathy, deeper understanding, and more effective communication lead to environments where innovation, collaboration, and personal development thrive. These effects, while individually subtle, collectively constitute a sea change in the dynamics of any group or organization.

By fostering environments where individuals feel understood and valued, Extreme Dialogue nurtures the seeds of transformation. This nurturing is not a one-time event but a continuous process that evolves, enhancing the capabilities of individuals to engage in meaningful, constructive dialogues. The importance of this nurturing process cannot be overstated, as it directly influences the quality and depth of personal and professional interactions.

To fully harness the potential of these principles, educators and coaches must not only integrate them into their practices but also embody them. It's that embodiment that serves as a living example to others, inspiring them to adopt and adapt these principles in their own lives.

Could the key to unlocking profound personal and professional growth lie in the way we talk to and understand each other?

Mastering Strategies for Advising Others

To truly guide others on their self-improvement journeys, it's essential to master strategies that leverage the principles of Extreme Dialogue effectively. This mastery involves not just understanding these principles at a theoretical level but living them out in every interaction. It demands a commitment to deep listening, empathy, and the fostering of a space where authentic dialogue can flourish.

Imagine guiding someone through a dense forest, where every step feels uncertain, and the path ahead is obscured. In this scenario, your role as a guide isn't merely to point out the direction but to provide a sense of safety and understanding that empowers the other person to navigate through the uncertainties themselves. This analogy captures the essence of advising others in their personal development journeys using Extreme Dialogue principles. It's about enabling them to find their path, equipped with the tools and confidence to face challenges head-on.

The deployment of these strategies often involves tailoring approaches to meet the unique needs and circumstances of each individual. This customization is where the depth of understanding and empathy comes into play, facilitating a bespoke journey of growth that respects the individual's pace and perspective. It's about crafting a narrative together, rather than prescribing a one-size-fits-all solution.

Ultimately, the capacity to guide others effectively hinges on the advisor's ability to remain open, curious, and committed to their own journey of growth. It's a reciprocal relationship where both parties learn and evolve, fueled by the principles of Extreme Dialogue.

The mastery of advising strategies within the framework of Extreme Dialogue creates a powerful dynamic that promotes personal growth for both the advisor and the advisee, bridging their journeys with empathy, understanding, and meaningful communication.

Incorporate Extreme Dialogue into your coaching and educational practices for powerful results. By embracing the principles outlined in this chapter, you have the opportunity to elevate your personal development efforts and those of your clients substantially. **Integrating these methodologies can lead to a multiplier effect, enhancing the impact of your guidance and advice.** Share these strategies with others to amplify their self-improvement journeys and contribute to meaningful transformations. **Master the art of advising others by leveraging these tools to unlock tangible success.** Empower yourself and those you coach with the tools to manifest goals with precision and clarity.

CHAPTER 9: THE ANALYTICAL MIND

Data-Centric Self-Improvement

> What if life itself could be the greatest data set we'd ever analyze?

Harnessing Data for Personal Growth

In an era where information is king, integrating data analysis with personal development isn't just innovative; it's essential. For individuals with a natural inclination towards data and evidence-based practices, the method of Extreme Dialogue offers a compelling framework. At its core, this approach is about making personal growth not just a goal but a measurable journey. By dissecting the appeal of Extreme Dialogue for data enthusiasts, we unlock a new dimension of self-improvement grounded in facts and figures.

Data analysis and personal development are more than mere companions; they are catalysts for each other. While personal development pushes one towards growth and self-actualization, data analysis offers the roadmap, marking milestones and highlighting areas for improvement. This synergy not only stimulates personal progress but also ensures that every step taken is informed and purposeful. Hence, understanding this relationship unveils a powerful tool for those keen on systematically advancing their personal and professional lives.

Learning strategies for applying a data-informed approach to personal growth is transformative. It's about transitioning from an abstract understanding of growth to a concrete, actionable plan. By leveraging metrics and analytics, individuals can set precise goals, track their progress, and refine strategies based on feedback loops. This process, inherently dynamic and iterative, promotes a culture of continuous improvement and lifelong learning.

What particularly stands out is **how Extreme Dialogue resonates with tech-savvy intellectuals and analysts**. This demographic, accustomed to navigating through vast datasets to extract meaningful insights, finds the structure and evidence-based nature of Extreme Dialogue not just appealing but intuitive. It aligns with their analytical mindset, driving engagement and fostering a deep commitment to applying this methodology across various life domains.

Moreover, within professional environments, advocating for data-informed personal growth practices encapsulates a broader shift towards efficiency, effectiveness, and accountability. It's a testament to the power of data in transforming not just businesses, but the individuals within them. Teams that embrace these practices witness not just enhanced performance, but a deeper sense of community and shared purpose, underscored by transparency, trust, and genuine connections.

Embracing Innovation, Creativity, and Intellectual Curiosity

In navigating the path of data-centric self-improvement, innovation and creativity are invaluable. Thinking outside the box and employing intellectual curiosity propel individuals beyond traditional limitations, enabling them to explore new territories in both personal and professional development. This exploration, grounded in data, not only validates one's journey but also illuminates possibilities previously unrealized.

Fostering genuine connections and transparent communication lies at the heart of this methodology. It's about building a framework where data does not overshadow human interaction but enhances it. By cultivating an environment where feedback is encouraged and growth is measured, individuals and teams alike can thrive.

To surmise, Extreme Dialogue advocates for a holistic, data-informed approach to personal growth, championing analytics as not just tools for business but for life. For those with a fervor for data, this chapter unveils a goldmine of strategies poised to refine personal development endeavors into a precise science. Engaging with these practices promises not just transformation but a perpetual journey towards excellence.

The Appealing Intersection of Extreme Dialogue for Data Lovers

In the realm of personal development, the marriage of data analysis and Extreme Dialogue emerges as a beacon of innovation to the analytically minded. For those intrigued by figures, statistics, and empirical evidence, the allure lies in the methodology's promise of tangible, measurable improvement. The process of Extreme Dialogue is not a mere abstract concept but a quantifiable journey, where each step forward can be tracked, analyzed, and enhanced.

Imagine trying to navigate a dense forest. Without a map or a compass, one relies on intuition, which, although valuable, often leads to wandering rather than a direct path to the destination. Extreme Dialogue for data enthusiasts is akin to navigating this forest with a GPS device, where each step is informed by data, reducing the guesswork and enhancing the likelihood of reaching the desired outcome efficiently.

This approach appeals deeply to those who prefer their decisions and developmental paths to be grounded in solid evidence. In a world inundated with fluctuating opinions and ephemeral trends, the data-driven nature of Extreme Dialogue provides a steady, reliable foundation. By integrating data analysis, individuals are equipped to make informed choices that lead to real, impactful change.

The structured nature of data analysis within personal growth also facilitates a deeper understanding of oneself. By quantifying behaviors, emotions, and outcomes, individuals gain insights into their own patterns, paving the way for a more profound and tailored approach to self-improvement. This introspection, guided by data, transforms personal development from a subjective endeavor into a scientific exploration.

The key appeal of Extreme Dialogue for data enthusiasts lies in its ability to transform the subjective journey of self-improvement into a measurable, data-driven process.

How Data Analysis Complements Personal Development

The synergy between data analysis and personal development might seem unconventional at first glance. Yet, upon closer inspection, it becomes clear that this combination is not only logical but also remarkably powerful. Data analysis involves sifting through information to unearth trends, patterns, and insights. Similarly, personal development requires an understanding of one's behaviors, habits, and reactions to foster growth and improvement.

The rhetorical power of data in our lives cannot be overstated. In professional settings, decisions are increasingly driven by data. Applying a similar approach to personal development is a logical extension. It represents a shift from relying solely on intuition to embracing a more empirical approach in charting one's growth journey.

Consider how a gardener tends to their garden. Without monitoring the health of the plants, their growth, and the effects of different environments, they can only hope for the best outcome. Data analysis in personal development functions similarly - it allows individuals to monitor their 'growth conditions', adapt strategies based on feedback, and cultivate a fertile ground for personal flourishing.

By intertwining data analysis with personal development, individuals unlock a new dimension of growth. This integration encourages a shift from a passive acceptance of one's state to an active role in shaping one's destiny. It empowers individuals to take charge of their growth, armed with insights gleaned from their data.

However, the true magic unfolds when this analytical approach leads to unexpected discoveries about oneself. The data collected might reveal hidden patterns, strengths, or areas for improvement that were previously obscured. It's akin to mining for gold - meticulous analysis can uncover valuable nuggets of self-awareness that, once polished, can significantly enhance one's quality of life.

But what might happen if we begin to view our personal growth journeys not just as paths to walk, but as treasure maps, with data as our compass?

The Data-Informed Personal Growth Framework (DIPGF)

Data Collection

The first step, *Data Collection*, is the cornerstone of the DIPGF. It's about systematically gathering information on our behaviors, emotions, and the outcomes of our actions. Think of it as setting up surveillance cameras in the museum of our lives. Every moment, action, and reaction is recorded for later analysis.

Whether it's through journaling, using digital apps, or leveraging wearable technology, the aim is to capture a comprehensive dataset that reflects one's daily life with precision.

Analysis & Insights

Subsequently, *Analysis & Insights* takes the spotlight. This phase is where the raw data collected transforms into actionable insights. Imagine sifting through a pile of puzzle pieces, each representing a piece of data. As the pieces come together, a clearer picture of oneself emerges. This can involve identifying triggers for certain emotions, understanding the impact of specific behaviors on one's productivity, or discerning patterns in decision-making processes. It's a deeply introspective phase that combines quantitative data with qualitative self-reflection, aiming to illuminate the areas ripe for development and growth.

Application

Finally, the *Application* phase is where the rubber meets the road. It's about taking the insights gleaned from the analysis and putting them into action. This step is akin to navigating a ship using the stars. The insights serve as a celestial map, guiding the journey of personal growth. Setting goals based on data, refining personal development strategies, and making informed decisions become the norm. Over time, this cyclical process of collecting data, analyzing it for insights, and applying those insights fosters a personalized, effective approach to personal development that evolves as the individual does.

The beauty of the DIPGF lies in its cyclical nature. It's not a linear journey but a spiral, where each cycle through the framework deepens one's understanding and refinement of personal growth strategies. Over time, as data accumulates and insights mature, individuals equipped with this framework can achieve a level of self-awareness and personal development that is deeply data-informed.

By embracing a structured, data-informed approach, individuals can unlock a deeper understanding of themselves, leading to more effective personal growth strategies.

In a world where data reigns supreme, the appeal of Extreme Dialogue for analytical minds is undeniable. The structured and data-centric approach to personal development resonates deeply with individuals who thrive on numbers, trends, and evidence. **For data enthusiasts, the marriage of data analysis with self-improvement is a match made in intellectual heaven.** The allure lies in the tangible results, the measurable progress, and the methodical nature of using data to drive personal growth.

By understanding how data analysis and personal development complement each other, individuals can unlock a new realm of possibilities. The synergy between these two seemingly different worlds opens doors to innovative strategies, precise decision-making, and continuous improvement. **Data-driven personal development offers a roadmap to success that is rooted in facts, figures, and informed choices.**

For those eager to apply a data-informed approach to personal growth, the key lies in strategic implementation and consistent evaluation. By setting clear goals, tracking progress, and adjusting strategies based on data insights, individuals can optimize their paths to success. **The journey towards self-improvement is not a random leap but a calculated progression guided by analytics and informed choices.**

Embrace the power of data in your personal development journey. Let the numbers guide you, the trends inspire you, and the evidence drive you towards your goals. With a data-centric mindset, you can turn aspirations into achievements, dreams into realities, and potential into performance. Elevate your self-improvement game by merging analytical prowess with personal growth strategies. Your success story awaits, backed by the strength of data and the clarity of purpose.

CHAPTER 10: A SELF-IMPROVEMENT ENTHUSIASTS GUIDE TO ACTIONABLE REALITY

Is it not in the space between dream and reality where life's most crucial steps are taken, where one learns to walk the ethereal bridge toward a horizon laced with the fruits of fulfillment?

Transform Stagnation into Dynamic Growth

The realm of personal development is fraught with abstract theories and well-meaning advice that often fall short in practical applicability. This gap between theory and practice represents a significant barrier to growth for many self-improvement enthusiasts aged 25-40. These individuals, deeply invested in their personal and professional advancement, urgently seek a bridge to connect their aspirations with tangible outcomes. **Extreme Dialogue**, a strategic approach to harnessing the power of conversation for actionable results, offers a structured pathway to navigate from personal stagnation to dynamic growth.

Navigating the journey from personal stagnation to dynamic growth requires a shift in perspective and strategy. Embracing **Extreme Dialogue** is not merely about engaging in conversations; it encompasses a strategic implementation of dialogue techniques to unlock profound insights and actions from everyday interactions. To effectively transition from a state of stagnation, it is crucial to identify the root causes of inertia. These often stem from a disconnect between one's aspirations and the actionable steps required to achieve them.

Implementing Extreme Dialogue strategies to bridge abstract concepts with real-world applications entails a deep dive into the mechanics of effective communication. This process involves refining the art of questioning, listening, and interpreting to extract actionable insights from dialogues. It's about moving beyond passive consumption of information and stepping into active engagement with ideas and concepts. By applying these strategies, individuals can distill complex ideas into practical steps that align with their personal growth trajectories.

Evaluating the alignment of personal aspirations with actionable pathways requires a methodical approach. It demands honest reflection on one's goals, strengths, and areas for improvement. Incorporating data-driven techniques, like growth hacking and analytics, enables individuals to measure progress accurately and adjust their strategies accordingly. This approach fosters a culture of continuous improvement, where data informs decision-making, propelling individuals towards their goals with precision and clarity.

The power of **teamwork and collaboration** cannot be overstated in this journey. Forming genuine relationships, built on trust and transparency, amplifies the impact of one's efforts. It creates a supportive ecosystem where ideas can flourish, innovation thrives, and goals are met with collective intelligence. Emphasizing the importance of networking within and outside one's industry fosters a dynamic environment conducive to growth and success.

Engaging with Extreme Dialogue is an invitation to think outside the box. It challenges individuals to push the boundaries of their creativity and intellectual curiosity. In the process, it opens doors to new opportunities and pathways for achievement that were previously obscured by conventional thinking. It's about fostering a mindset that welcomes change, embraces challenges, and continually seeks out ways to refine and reframe one's approach to personal and professional development.

In essence, the transition from dialogue to actionable reality is a transformative journey of embracing innovation, fostering genuine connections, and applying structured strategies to bridge the gap between aspirations and achievements. By harnessing the power of Extreme Dialogue, self-improvement enthusiasts can unlock a world of opportunities, turning their words into wins and manifesting success with precision, clarity, and confidence. This strategic approach not only propels individuals towards their goals but also cultivates an environment of continuous growth and development, where every conversation holds the potential to unlock actionable insights and pave the way for tangible advancements.

Navigating From Stagnation to Growth

Personal stagnation feels like being caught in quicksand; no matter how hard you struggle, it seems impossible to break free. Yet, it is the first step in a transformative journey toward dynamic growth. Understanding why we feel stuck is crucial. Often, it boils down to comfort zones, fear of failure, or simply not knowing which direction to take. Recognizing these barriers is the key to overcoming them.

Imagine your growth as a garden. In the beginning, it's just a plot of land—barren, untouched. It's your actions, like planting seeds and consistently tending to them, that transform it into a thriving garden. Similarly, personal growth requires initiative and consistent effort. It's about making the decision to step out of the quicksand and planting your feet on solid ground.

The process of moving from stagnation to growth is neither

linear nor predictable. It involves trial and error, facing setbacks, and learning from them. This adaptive process is what builds resilience and fosters a growth mindset. Each challenge overcome is a step out of the quicksand, each lesson learned a seed planted in your garden of growth.

To effectively navigate this journey, setting clear, achievable goals is essential. These goals act as signposts, guiding you through the fog of uncertainty. Without them, it's easy to veer off path or, worse, remain stuck in the same spot. Embracing change, seeking new experiences, and being open to learning are also fundamental in evolving from a state of stagnation to one of dynamic growth.

In essence, breaking free from stagnation and embracing dynamic growth is about recognizing barriers, setting clear goals, and consistently working towards them.

Implementing Extreme Dialogue Strategies

Extreme Dialogue, a methodical approach to tying theoretical concepts with practical life applications, promises a bridge for translating vague ideas into concrete actions. It starts with understanding that theory without application is like a ship without a sail; it might have the potential to move but lacks direction. Extreme Dialogue offers that direction.

Let's frame Extreme Dialogue strategies as a toolbox. Each tool serves a unique purpose in crafting your reality from abstract ideas. For instance, active listening and open questioning are tools for mining deeper insights, while structured reflection helps in aligning these insights with personal values and goals.

Powerful stories and testimonies serve as proof of concept, showing the real-world effectiveness of the strategies. These narratives are not just inspiring; they're practical blueprints. They demonstrate how others have successfully navigated challenges, providing a roadmap you can modify to suit your journey.

Deploying Extreme Dialogue effectively requires a shift in perspective—viewing every interaction as an opportunity to learn and every challenge as a chance to apply theoretical knowledge. This mindset shift is crucial for connecting abstract concepts with practical applications.

Analogously, think of Extreme Dialogue as translating a complex musical score into a melody. The score—abstract, full of symbols and instructions—holds potential. But it's the musician, through their instrument, who brings this potential to life in form of melodies that can move, inspire, and even induce change. Similarly, Extreme Dialogue is the instrument that plays the abstract scores of concepts into the harmonious melody of actionable reality.

What if the missing piece in bridging theory and practice was merely a change in perspective, facilitated by Extreme Dialogue?

Aligning Aspirations with Actionable Pathways

Personal aspirations are like stars in the night sky—they light up our dreams and guide our journeys. However, turning these aspirations into reality requires finding a pathway through the darkness. It's about connecting the dots between where we are and where we wish to be. This third objective is crucial: evaluating the alignment of our dreams with actionable pathways.

To start, it's essential to clearly define your aspirations. Be as specific as possible. Wanting to improve your life is a noble goal, but it's too nebulous. What area of your life do you want to improve? What does improvement look like? Concrete goals are like lighthouses in the night; they give direction and purpose to our efforts.

Next, comes the analysis—comparing your current situation with your end goals. It's like mapping a route before embarking on a journey. Consider what skills, resources, and changes are needed to bridge the gap. This step often reveals much about the feasibility of dreams and what it truly takes to achieve them.

Implementing a plan is the bridge between aspirations and achievements. It's breaking down the journey into manageable steps, adjusting strategies as needed, and actively moving forward. Imagine a gardener nurturing their garden. Just as they adjust their strategies based on the plant's growth, weather, and unforeseen challenges, so must we adapt our approaches to align our pathways with our aspirations.

Analogously, aligning aspirations with actionable pathways is like tracing a constellation in the sky. While each star may shine on its own, it's only by connecting them with lines (our actions and plans) that we reveal the hidden picture (our aspirations made reality).

Aligning aspirations with actionable pathways is about defining clear goals, making a realistic evaluation, and taking decisive action towards realization. This process not only bridges the gap between where we are and where we wish to be but also ensures that our journey is guided by the stars of our true desires.

Going Beyond Aspirations

Bridge the gap between where you are and where you want to be. Take charge of your personal growth journey by embracing actionable strategies that transform your dreams into reality. *Implement Extreme Dialogue techniques* to bring clarity to your aspirations and chart a course towards tangible success. The journey from stagnation to growth is within your reach when you align your goals with practical pathways.

Embracing Practicality

Connect theory with practice for concrete results. Dive deep into the realm of self-improvement with a focus on real-world applications. *Evaluate the alignment* of your desires with actionable steps to ensure that your efforts lead to meaningful achievements. Transform abstract concepts into actionable plans that propel you towards your ultimate goals.

Catalyst for Advancement

Unleash your potential with structured guidance. Amplify your journey of self-discovery and personal development through the power of actionable reality. *Navigate the process* of growth with precision and purpose, leveraging Extreme Dialogue to steer your aspirations towards actualization. Embrace the actionable nature of this approach to propel yourself towards fulfillment and success.

CHAPTER 11: THE DATA-DRIVEN PROFESSIONAL'S BLUEPRINT

If data informs the potential within our professional pursuits, what untapped insights lurk within life's vast, uncharted personal relationships?

Unlock the Power of Data in Your Professional Journey

In today's fast-paced world, professionals in the age bracket of 30-45 are continuously seeking novel strategies to leverage their careers and personal development. The *Data-Driven Professional's Blueprint* charts a course through the integration of a structured, data-informed approach in harmony with Extreme Dialogue principles. This path not only optimizes decision-making and efficacy but also polishes personal interrelations and growth. Recognizing the immense potential of a data-driven mindset, this chapter provides actionable insights into transforming analytical proficiency into tangible success.

Harnessing an analytical mindset is not merely about crunching numbers or navigating spreadsheets. It's about **seeing the patterns in data that others overlook**, and implementing these insights to forecast, plan, and achieve unprecedented outcomes. The chapter opens by illustrating how transforming your mindset to think analytically empowers you to decode complex scenarios, anticipate challenges, and spearhead initiatives that lead to personal and professional optimization. This strategic pivot is not about adding more to your workload but about working smarter, where every decision is backed by data.

Integration of Extreme Dialogue principles with data analytics brings about a revolutionary approach to tackling projects and tasks. It's not just about what the data tells you; it's about asking the right questions. **Dialogue plays a crucial role in this process**, fostering an environment where ideas can be shared openly and strategies can be refined with precision. This chapter guides readers on utilizing these principles to enhance informed decision-making, thereby boosting productivity. It equips professionals with the tools to dissect and digest data, ensuring that their actions and decisions are both informed and impactful.

Moreover, a structured, data-informed approach emerges as a powerful navigational tool in the interpersonal sphere of one's professional journey. This isn't about reducing human interactions to numbers; rather, it's about **understanding the dynamics and patterns** that lead to more meaningful connections and growth opportunities. Through real-world examples and case studies, the chapter demonstrates how data can illuminate pathways to fostering genuine relationships, building trust, and achieving transparency in all professional engagements.

Collaboration and teamwork are emphasized as foundational pillars for success in any data-driven endeavor. By advocating for the creation of cohesive teams where diverse skills and perspectives converge, the chapter underscores the importance of collective intelligence in achieving goals. It offers strategies for leveraging data in team settings, ensuring that every member is aligned and motivated towards common objectives.

Innovation and creativity are also hallmarks of the data-driven professional. Moving beyond the conventional, this chapter prompts readers to **think outside the box**, applying their analytical skills to discover unique solutions and navigate uncharted territories in their industries. By fostering intellectual curiosity, it encourages professionals to explore new avenues where data acts as both a compass and a catalyst for groundbreaking ideas.

The insights provided herein are not just theoretical musings but are backed by industry-specific vocabulary and examples from fields such as growth hacking, content creation, and marketing strategy. This not only adds credibility but makes the content tangible and directly applicable to the reader's own context.

Transforming Analysis into Action

Ultimately, this chapter serves as a blueprint for the data-driven professional keen on navigating the complex interplay of data, dialogue, and decision-making. Through a blend of analytics and human insight, individuals are equipped to make informed decisions, inspire innovation in their teams, and foster genuine relationships that propel personal and professional growth. Whether you're a marketer, growth hacker, or content creator, the insights offered promise a transformational journey from dialogue to tangible success, making your words truly translate into wins.

Harnessing an analytical mindset is not just about crunching numbers or being good with data; it is about applying a structured, critical thinking process to every decision and challenge. Think of it as using a map to navigate through a city. You could explore without direction, or you could use the map to find the best route, avoid traffic, and reach your destination more efficiently. Similarly, an analytical mindset helps you navigate the complex landscape of personal and professional challenges with more clarity and precision.

The key to leveraging an analytical mindset lies in consistently questioning assumptions, evaluating evidence, and considering outcomes. This approach to thinking ensures that decisions are not made on a whim but are the result of careful consideration and analysis of the available data. It is about being curious, asking the right questions, and using the answers to inform your choices. Remember, the goal is optimization – doing better today than you did yesterday, in every aspect of your life.

Just as a gardener tills the soil, plants the seeds, and nurtures the growth to harvest the fruits, you too must prepare your mind, sow the seeds of knowledge and critical thinking, and cultivate your skills to reap the benefits of personal and professional growth. An analytical mindset is your toolset in this endeavor, helping you to analyze your actions, refine your strategies, and measure your progress. It's about making informed decisions that steer you closer to your goals, whether that's improving career prospects, enhancing personal relationships, or achieving financial stability.

Implementing an analytical mindset requires a shift in perspective. You start to see challenges not as obstacles but as opportunities to gather data, analyze, and iterate. It demands a proactive approach, constantly seeking out information, analyzing trends, and anticipating outcomes to stay ahead. This mindset is not inherited; it is built through practice and dedication. By embracing an analytical approach, you empower yourself to navigate the complexities of life with confidence and precision.

In essence, the power of an analytical mindset lies in its capacity to transform challenges into opportunities for optimization and growth.

Integrate Extreme Dialogue Principles for Informed Decision-Making and Productivity Improvement

The principles of Extreme Dialogue champion a transformative approach to communication, marked by intentionality, clarity, and purpose. It's not merely about talking; it's about engaging in conversations that drive action and result in measurable outcomes. Think of it as the difference between shooting arrows in the dark hoping to hit a target and using a laser-sighted bow under the guidance of a skilled archer. The principles of Extreme Dialogue ensure that your efforts are directed, intentional, and yield tangible results.

Implementing these principles requires a conscious effort to listen actively, to speak with purpose, and to seek understanding in every interaction. It is akin to laying down a two-way street where information and insights flow freely, permitting a more profound connection and mutual respect to emerge. This approach fosters an environment where decisions are not just top-down directives but collaborative efforts informed by diverse perspectives.

Building on the foundation of an analytical mindset, the principles of Extreme Dialogue encourage a data-informed approach to decision-making. This approach is characterized by gathering relevant information, weighing options based on evidence, and choosing paths that are most likely to lead to successful outcomes. It's a disciplined process that combines intuition with intellect, ensuring that productivity is not a matter of chance but a predictable result of informed actions.

Visualization techniques can be especially powerful in applying Extreme Dialogue principles effectively. Imagine mapping out a conversation as you would a journey, identifying where you are, where you need to go, and what obstacles might arise along the way. By anticipating challenges and preparing your responses, you ensure that the dialogue remains constructive and on course towards achieving your objectives.

In the realm of productivity, the combination of analytical

thinking and Extreme Dialogue can be revolutionary. It shifts the focus from being busy to being effective, from doing more to doing better. By making every action and conversation count, you multiply your effectiveness and accelerate your progress towards your goals.

Could integrating Extreme Dialogue into your daily routine be the key to unlocking unprecedented growth and efficiency?

Apply a Structured, Data-Informed Approach to Navigate Interpersonal Relationships and Growth

Interpersonal relationships are often seen as the realm of emotion, intuition, and personal connection. However, adopting a structured, data-informed approach can significantly enhance the quality and depth of these relationships. Imagine if, like a gardener knows the specific needs of each plant, you could understand and cater to the needs of the people around you with that same level of detail and care. By gathering 'data' on their preferences, communication styles, and boundaries, you can forge deeper, more meaningful connections.

This approach does not mean treating relationships like a science experiment. Rather, it's about being mindful and intentional in your interactions, noticing patterns, and adjusting your behavior accordingly. It's recognizing when to offer support, when to challenge, and when to step back, based on an understanding of the other person's needs and your shared history. This tailored approach makes every interaction more meaningful and effective, helping to build trust and mutual respect.

Combining the principles of Extreme Dialogue with a data-informed mindset transforms how we communicate in personal and professional contexts. It involves actively listening, processing the information shared, and responding in ways that affirm the other's perspective, even when you disagree. This level of empathy and understanding can significantly impact the dynamics of a relationship, promoting a culture of open, honest, and productive communication.

In navigating growth, whether personal or professional, a structured, data-informed approach offers a clear advantage. It allows you to set specific, measurable goals, track your progress, and adapt your strategies based on feedback. Success, in this context, becomes not just a possibility but an expectation. You are no longer navigating the unpredictable currents of change blindly but steering your ship with precision, guided by the stars of data and insight.

By weaving together an analytical mindset, the principles of Extreme Dialogue, and a structured, data-informed approach, we unlock a powerful blueprint for navigating life's challenges. This synergy not only enhances personal and professional growth but also enriches our interactions, making every conversation a stepping stone towards achieving our highest potential.

Embrace the Power of Data-Driven Practices

The key to unlocking your full potential lies in embracing the power of data-driven practices. **Harness your analytical mindset** to optimize your personal and professional growth. By integrating Extreme Dialogue principles, you pave the way for informed decision-making and productivity improvement.

Elevate Decision-Making with Intentional Dialogue

Integrate Extreme Dialogue principles into your decision-making processes. Let data be your guiding light, illuminating the path to success. Combine strategic thinking with thoughtful communication to drive positive outcomes in both your personal and professional endeavors.

Foster Growth through Data-Informed Relationships

Apply a structured, data-informed approach to nurture your interpersonal relationships. Cultivate authenticity, transparency, and trust to foster genuine connections that fuel growth. By prioritizing data-driven practices in your interactions, you pave the way for meaningful progress and lasting success.

Drive Success through Strategic Integration

The Data-Driven Professional's Blueprint serves as your roadmap to success. By intertwining an analytical mindset with the principles of Extreme Dialogue, you position yourself for unparalleled growth and achievement. Embrace this structured approach to maximize your potential and turn your aspirations into reality.

CHAPTER 12: THE PROGRESSIVE MENTOR & EDUCATOR

Shaping the Thinkers of Tomorrow

Unlocking the Minds of Tomorrow

In a world saturated with information and rapidly shifting societal landscapes, the role of education has never been more critical. It stands as a beacon of hope and a tool for preparing the thinkers of tomorrow. This reality has birthed a new paradigm in teaching methodologies—one that transcends traditional lecture-based lessons in favor of fostering deep, critical thinking and nuanced communication skills among students. At the heart of this evolution lies the method of Extreme Dialogue —an innovative approach that prioritizes self-reflection, clear communication, and intentional dialogue. Specializing in this method, the Progressive Educator avatar emerges as a champion for nurturing holistic development in learners, making them adept at navigating the complexities of the modern world.

Educators, particularly those aged 35-50 who are keen on integrating cutting-edge teaching strategies, will find in Extreme Dialogue a treasure trove of techniques designed to elevate their students' learning experience. By focusing on critical thinking, these educators can ignite a spark of curiosity and encourage a deeper engagement with the material. To harness the full potential of this method, identifying specific strategies to foster critical thinking and engagement becomes imperative.

Integrating Extreme Dialogue into educational practices isn't merely about enhancing academic skills; it's about facilitating holistic development. This involves sculpting individuals who are not only academically proficient but also emotionally intelligent and capable of thoughtful, meaningful interactions. Such holistic development equips students with a well-rounded skill set essential for success in both personal and professional spheres.

Key to this holistic evolution is mastering the art of self-reflection and intentional dialogue. In the bustling pace of today's world, the ability to pause, reflect, and engage in meaningful dialogue is invaluable. It aids students in understanding their thoughts, emotions, and the world around them more clearly, fostering a sense of empathy and community. The role of the educator, therefore, extends beyond teaching to empowering—guiding students in unlocking their potential to learn, grow, and thrive.

Reflection Revolution: A Step by Step Guide to Enlightening Education

Step 1: Establish a classroom environment that champions self-reflection. This necessitates the creation of a space where students feel respected and safe to express themselves freely. This is the cornerstone of fostering a culture of openness and introspection.

Step 2: Introduce students to a variety of self-reflection techniques. This could range from journaling and mindfulness exercises to guided self-reflection prompts. Providing clear, practical examples can significantly enhance the efficacy of these techniques.

Step 3: Incorporate reflection activities seamlessly into lesson plans. Assignments, projects, and even daily lessons should be punctuated with moments dedicated to introspection, encouraging students to examine their learning journey critically.

Step 4: Utilize guiding questions to deepen the reflection process. Encouraging students to explore beyond the surface with questions like, "What did you learn about yourself?" or "How has this challenged your beliefs or assumptions?" can lead to profound insights and growth.

Step 5: Facilitate peer and group reflection sessions. Structured discussions among students can offer diverse perspectives and promote empathy, adding a valuable dimension to the learning experience.

Step 6: As an educator, model self-reflection with honesty and transparency. Sharing personal experiences and growth instances can inspire students to embrace self-reflection more openly and earnestly.

Step 7: Provide targeted feedback and guidance throughout the self-reflection process. Constructive feedback that highlights strengths and areas for improvement can help sharpen students' self-awareness and guide their personal development journey.

Step 8: Dedicate time explicitly for reflection. Whether through journals, group discussions, or quiet contemplation, making reflection a regular part of the schedule reinforces its importance and benefits.

Step 9: Connect the dots between self-reflection and its real-world applications. Demonstrating how reflective practices can enhance decision-making, personal growth, and social interactions can make the process more relevant and compelling for students.

Step 10: Finally, celebrate growth and recognize achievements. Fostering a culture that values effort and progress over perfection can motivate students to continue on their path of self-improvement and discovery.

Empowering students through Extreme Dialogue not only

enriches their academic journey but also prepares them to face the world with confidence, empathy, and a deep-seated understanding of themselves and others. The transformation from passive receivers of information to active, engaged thinkers is a testament to the power of education shaped by dialogue, reflection, and holistic development. As educators harness these tools, they light the way for generations to come, shaping the thinkers of tomorrow.

Fostering Critical Thinking and Engagement

In today's rapidly evolving world, the ability for students to think critically and engage deeply with content is more important than ever. Critical thinking, at its core, involves analyzing facts to form a judgment. It's not just about thinking more deeply but also about challenging assumptions, including one's own. This skill allows individuals to navigate complex issues efficiently, making it a cornerstone of education that aims to prepare students for the complexities of the modern world.

Imagine a garden. Just as diverse plants need different nutrients to grow, students require varied methods to foster their critical thinking. Traditional lecture-based learning might work for some, but others thrive on group discussions, hands-on projects, or multimedia resources. By diversifying teaching methods, educators can cater to the unique learning styles of their students, much like how a skilled gardener tends to each plant's specific needs. This approach not only engages students but also encourages them to explore and apply their learning in real-life contexts.

One effective method to foster critical thinking is through question-based learning. By challenging students with open-ended questions, educators encourage them to think beyond textbook answers and dive deeper into subjects. This process cultivates a classroom environment where inquiry is welcome, fostering a culture of curiosity and engagement. When students are encouraged to ask questions and seek out their answers, they develop the confidence and skills to critically assess information, a crucial ability in today's information-saturated environment.

Another key strategy is the incorporation of real-world problems into the curriculum. When students see the direct application of their studies to real-world scenarios, their engagement and interest in learning deepen. Solving actual problems requires them to apply critical thinking and creativity, thereby solidifying their understanding and application of knowledge. Through these practical applications, education becomes not just about memorization but about the meaningful application of knowledge to real-life situations.

To nurture critical thinkers, educators must diversify teaching methods, encourage questions, and connect learning to the real world.

Nurturing Self-Reflection in Education

Finding innovative ways to integrate self-reflection in education is pivotal for holistic development. Self-reflection enables students to consider their learning experiences thoughtfully, understand their strengths and weaknesses, and set personal growth goals. Extreme Dialogue, as a method, lends itself well to fostering this kind of introspection and development.

Consider the metaphor of a journey. Just as travelers must occasionally stop to assess their direction, reflect on the experiences gathered, and plan their next steps, students, too, need structured opportunities to pause and reflect on their educational journey. This process of ongoing self-evaluation and reflection is crucial for personal growth and learning.

The Reflective Pathway: A 10-Step Guide to Integrating Self-Reflection

Create a Safe and Supportive Learning Environment

Establishing a classroom atmosphere where students feel secure to express themselves and share their thoughts is foundational. A nurturing environment acts as fertile soil that allows the seeds of reflection to sprout and take root.

Introduce Self-Reflection Techniques

Whether it's journaling, mindfulness, or guided prompts, familiarizing students with different reflection methods provides them with the tools they need to embark on their introspective journey.

Incorporate Reflection Activities into Lessons

Allocating time for reflection after activities links learning with personal insight, turning every lesson into an opportunity for self-discovery.

Provide Guiding Questions

Questions like "What did you learn about yourself?" act as signposts, guiding students through the terrain of their own minds and encouraging deeper exploration.

Foster Peer and Group Reflection

Sharing reflections builds a community of learners, where insights are shared, and diverse perspectives are valued.

Model Self-Reflection

By sharing your own reflections, you light the way, showing students that the reflective journey is one of ongoing growth and learning.

Provide Feedback and Guidance

Constructive feedback serves as a compass, helping students

navigate their thoughts and reflections towards meaningful insights.

Make Time for Reflection

Dedicated reflection time is a clear statement of the value placed on this practice, ensuring it becomes a habit rather than an afterthought.

Connect Reflection to Real-Life Applications

Linking reflection to real-world scenarios bridges the gap between theory and practice, making learning relevant and impactful.

Celebrate Growth and Achievements

Recognizing progress on this reflective journey fuels motivation, inspiring ongoing engagement with the process.

What might change if reflection became as integral to education as learning itself?

Equipping Students for the Modern World

In an age where information is at our fingertips, the ability to critically assess this information and reflect on one's perspectives is invaluable. Equipping students with self-reflection and intentional dialogue skills prepares them for the complexities and challenges of the modern world.

Just like a navigator uses a compass to find their way in uncharted territory, students use self-reflection to navigate their learning and personal growth. Intentional dialogue acts as the map, guiding conversations that are meaningful and purpose-driven. Together, these skills empower students to understand their thinking processes, communicate effectively, and make informed decisions.

Developing these skills requires practice and intention. By

engaging in thoughtful dialogue, whether in classroom discussions, team projects, or peer feedback sessions, students hone their ability to think critically and communicate their ideas clearly. Through self-reflection, they gain insights into their own biases, beliefs, and values, enabling them to approach conversations and conflicts with empathy and understanding.

Moreover, these skills are not confined to the academic world. They are essential for thriving in the workplace, contributing to society, and fostering healthy relationships. By encouraging students to question, analyze, and reflect, educators prepare them for a lifetime of learning and adaptation.

By fostering critical thinking, integrating self-reflection, and teaching intentional dialogue, Progressive Educators equip students with essential skills for navigating the complexities of the modern world.

Embracing Innovative Education Methods

As educators, it is imperative to **embrace innovative methods** that foster critical thinking, engagement, and holistic development in students. The utilization of Extreme Dialogue can revolutionize the way we shape the thinkers of tomorrow. By integrating **this approach into educational practices**, we are creating a powerful foundation for students to thrive in the modern world.

Equipping Students for Success

The tools we provide our students today will shape the leaders of tomorrow. Through fostering **self-reflection and intentional dialogue skills**, we are equipping them with the essential competencies needed to navigate the complexities of the contemporary landscape. As Progressive Educators, it is our responsibility to empower our students with the skills necessary to excel in a rapidly evolving society.

A Call to Action

Let us rally behind the belief that **education is the key to transformation**. By integrating Extreme Dialogue practices, we can steer our students towards a future brimming with possibilities. The time is now to equip our learners with the tools to think critically, communicate effectively, and engage meaningfully. As Progressive Educators, let us pave the way for a generation that is not only knowledgeable but also adept at navigating the challenges and opportunities that lie ahead.

CHAPTER 13: CONSCIOUSLY CREATING FAMILIAL BONDS

The Art of Thoughtful Engagement

Unlock the Power of Thoughtful Engagement

In a world where every word and action shapes our children's future, mastering the art of communication is not just an option —it's a necessity. The concept of Extreme Dialogue, a method designed to enhance communication strategies exponentially, holds the key to transforming how we connect with our loved ones, especially our children. This approach, centered on **deep connections, thoughtful engagement, and balance between personal growth and parenting**, offers a strategic pathway for parents dedicated to fostering emotional intelligence and resilience in their offspring.

The essence of Extreme Dialogue lies in its ability to elevate conversations beyond the superficial. It's not just about talking; it's about engaging in a manner that encourages both parties to listen actively, respond thoughtfully, and empathize deeply. For parents, this means stepping into conversations with their children with an open heart and mind, ready to explore their worldviews without judgment. This practice paves the way for **authentic connections**, laying a solid foundation for mutual respect and understanding.

Moreover, applying Extreme Dialogue principles in everyday interactions serves a dual purpose. It not only enhances our communication skills but also models exemplary behavior for our children. By witnessing their parents engage thoughtfully with the world, children learn the importance of considering diverse perspectives, cultivating empathy, and navigating challenges with grace. This form of role modeling is instrumental in nurturing young minds that are equipped to deal with life's complexities with resilience and openness.

Balancing personal growth with effective parenting is a critical aspect that this chapter delves into. It articulates strategies that enable parents to pursue their aspirations while ensuring their parenting style remains engaged, responsive, and attuned to their children's needs. This balance is essential for maintaining a healthy and supportive family environment where every member feels valued and understood.

Embracing Extreme Dialogue offers a roadmap to becoming a Conscious Parent, one who recognizes the profound impact of their words and actions on their children's development. This approach encourages parents to cultivate a communication style that promotes deep connections, supports personal and familial growth, and exemplifies thoughtful engagement with the wider world.

Through the lenses of metrics, analytics, and data analysis, we see the tangible benefits of adopting Extreme Dialogue in the realm of parenting. Increased emotional intelligence, improved conflict resolution skills, and stronger parent-child relationships are just the tip of the iceberg. These outcomes not only enrich family life but also equip our children with the skills to navigate their future with confidence and compassion.

In essence, the journey to becoming a Conscious Parent through Extreme Dialogue is a transformative one. It invites us to refine our communication skills, deepen our connections, and model the thoughtful engagement we wish to see in the world. As we embark on this journey, we unlock the potential to foster a generation that is emotionally intelligent, resilient, and equipped to turn dialogue into meaningful reality.

In today's rapidly evolving world, connecting with our children on a deeper level is more important than ever before. With distractions from technology, the hustle of daily life, and the pressure to "do it all," parents are seeking ways to bridge communication gaps. Mastering communication techniques that foster deep connections with children is not just beneficial; it's crucial.

Imagine if each conversation with your child was like carefully planting seeds in a garden. Just as the right environment, nurturing, and patience can transform seeds into thriving plants, the right communication strategies can cultivate a strong and healthy relationship with your children.

It starts with active listening, a skill often overlooked in our fast-paced environment. Active listening involves giving your full attention to your child, without distractions, and responding in a way that makes them feel understood and valued. This cultivates an environment of trust, where your child feels safe to share their thoughts and feelings.

Following this, is the practice of open-ended questioning. Instead of yes or no questions, open-ended questions encourage deeper conversation and thinking. They prompt your child to share more about their experiences and perspectives, providing a window into their world.

Imagine now, the seeds you've planted have begun to sprout. These sprouts represent the growing trust and understanding between you and your child, nurtured by your attentive communication techniques.

To summarize, mastering communication techniques that foster deep connections involves active listening and open-ended questioning, akin to planting seeds in a fertile garden.

Applying Extreme Dialogue Principles

Incorporating Extreme Dialogue principles into our daily interactions can significantly change how we engage with the world - and most importantly, with our children. These principles aren't just communication tools; they're a mindset shift. They help us model behaviors of thoughtful engagement, showcasing empathy, openness, and understanding.

Rhetorically speaking, how often do we practice what we preach in front of our children? Extreme Dialogue encourages us to walk the talk. It's about demonstrating the qualities we wish to instill in our kids, such as resilience, patience, and active listening.

The methodology of Extreme Dialogue underscores the value of reflective questioning. It involves pausing to consider the impact of our words and actions, and asking ourselves if they align with the values we aim to convey. This introspection can significantly enrich our interactions with our children and those around us.

Imagine your family interactions as a dance. In dancing, each step, movement, and gesture is intentional, contributing to the dance's overall beauty and harmony. Similarly, Extreme Dialogue guides us to be intentional in our words and actions, ensuring they contribute positively to the fabric of our relationships.

Extreme Dialogue also emphasizes the importance of feedback - giving and receiving it constructively. By modeling this with our children, we foster a culture of open communication, where feedback is seen as a tool for growth rather than criticism.

This leads us to a pertinent question: **What if the secret to deeper familial bonds lies in our capacity to model the principles of Extreme Dialogue, showcasing empathy, intentionality, and thoughtful feedback?**

Exploring Strategies for Balancing Personal Growth with Effective Parenting

The Conscious Engagement Framework (CEF) offers a holistic approach to fostering deep connections through thoughtful communication and engagement.

Mindful Communication

The cornerstone of CEF is Mindful Communication. This involves not only listening to what is being said but how it's said, and what might not be said at all. It encourages parents to communicate with empathy and understanding, creating a safe space for children to express themselves freely. This pillar supports the mutual growth of both parent and child by fostering an environment of open dialogue and trust. *Mindful Communication* transforms simple conversations into opportunities for connection and learning.

Intentional Action

The next pillar, Intentional Action, is about aligning our actions with our values. It requires us to think critically about the example we set for our children. Every action - whether it's how we manage stress, interact with others, or approach challenges - sends a powerful message to our kids. By applying the principles of Extreme Dialogue to our actions, we model behaviors that we wish our children to adopt, such as patience, resilience, and thoughtfulness.

Reflective Feedback

Finally, we have Reflective Feedback. This pillar champions the idea of mutual growth through open discussions about thoughts, behaviors, and emotions. It encourages parents and children alike to reflect on their actions and the impact they have. By providing and encouraging constructive feedback, we foster a culture of continuous learning and adaptation, strengthening the bond between parent and child.

The Conscious Engagement Framework (CEF) operates much like a garden ecosystem, where Mindful Communication, Intentional Action, and Reflective Feedback interact symbiotically. Each component depends on and reinforces the others, creating a dynamic and nurturing environment conducive to growth.

In practice, CEF encourages us to reflect on our behaviors and attitudes regularly, ensuring they align with the values we wish to instill in our children. It transforms the challenging balancing act of personal growth and effective parenting into a journey of mutual development and understanding.

In weaving together masterful communication, the application of Extreme Dialogue principles, and the Conscious Engagement Framework, we find a powerful approach to not just being better parents but growing alongside our children.

In mastering communication techniques that foster deep connections with our children, there is a profound opportunity to shape their emotional intelligence and resilience for life. By modeling thoughtful engagement with the world through Extreme Dialogue principles, we set a powerful example that transcends mere words and transforms into tangible actions. **Balancing personal growth with effective parenting is not just a goal; it's a journey of continuous learning and reflection.** As Conscious Parents, we have the chance to inspire curiosity, creativity, and authenticity in ourselves and our children, creating a legacy of meaningful connections that endure beyond the present moment.

CHAPTER 14: THE TRANSFORMATIVE JOURNEY

Crafting Reality Through Conversation

> Our thoughts and conversations today will not merely pass through time—they will shape it.

Transform Your Words into Wins

Empowering individuals to sculpt their reality through intentional conversation and self-reflection, Extreme Dialogue stands as a beacon in the digital era, where thoughts are not merely abstract, but the seeds of our future reality. At the core of this transformative journey is the recognition that the language we use and the conversations we engage in play a foundational role in shaping our personal and professional landscapes. **Extreme Dialogue harnesses the power of strategic, data-informed conversations**, merging mindset with metric analysis to foster personal and professional growth.

In an age inundated with information, the approach of Extreme Dialogue is not just revolutionary but necessary. It transcends traditional dialogue techniques by incorporating real-time data analytics, enabling individuals to make informed decisions and steer conversations towards desired outcomes. This methodology doesn't just theorize success; it maps out a practical path to turning abstract dreams into tangible achievements. By advocating for this intentional and analytical conversation strategy, individuals are equipped to navigate the complexities of the digital age with precision and foresight.

The transformative power of Extreme Dialogue is rooted in its ability to bridge the gap between a positive mindset and tangible outcomes. Many individuals understand the importance of maintaining a positive mindset yet struggle to manifest their aspirations into reality. Extreme Dialogue offers a solution, providing a clear framework for moving from ideation to realization. By engaging in data-informed conversations, individuals can dissect their ambitions, understand their underlying components, and devise a strategy grounded in reality, not just optimism.

The synergy between mindset and data is not just about achieving personal milestones; it's a comprehensive strategy that extends to professional success. In the professional world, where competition is fierce and the margin for error is slim, the principles of Extreme Dialogue can be the differentiator. By fostering genuine connections, trust, and transparency in professional engagements, individuals and teams can unlock a higher level of innovation, creativity, and productivity. The methodology champions the formation of authentic relationships, encouraging collaboration and mutual growth.

Moreover, Extreme Dialogue emphasizes the importance of self-reflection in this transformative journey. Beyond external conversations, engaging in intentional dialogue with oneself is crucial. This internal conversation, informed by data and introspection, allows individuals to align their actions with their goals, ensuring that every step taken is one towards actualization of their dreams.

As we delve deeper into the digital age, the need for innovative approaches to personal and professional development becomes increasingly clear. Extreme Dialogue, with its foundation in intentional, data-informed conversation, offers a fresh perspective on the art of manifestation. It empowers individuals to not only dream but to meticulously craft their reality, turning thoughts and words into wins.

In essence, Extreme Dialogue is more than a methodology; it's a journey towards mastery of the self and the external world. By recognizing the power of our thoughts and language, employing intentional conversations informed by data, and understanding the transformative potential of this approach, individuals are poised to navigate the path from dialogue to reality. This journey, rich with personal growth and professional achievement, encapsulates the spirit of Extreme Dialogue—transforming the abstract into the tangible, one conversation at a time.

Recognize the Foundational Role of Thoughts and Language in Shaping Personal Reality

The notion that our thoughts and the language we use can fundamentally transform our reality is not merely poetic; it's powerfully pragmatic. At the heart of this principle is the understanding that what we think and speak directly influences what we perceive as possible, ultimately shaping our actions and outcomes. It's a concept mirrored in disciplines across philosophy, psychology, and even quantum physics, suggesting that our mental and verbal expressions play a crucial role in the manifestation of our personal and professional lives.

Consider the analogy of a garden. Just as the seeds we plant determine the kinds of plants that grow, the thoughts we nurture and the words we utter shape the reality that unfolds before us. If we plant seeds of doubt and speak words of negativity, we cultivate an environment where success is stifled. Conversely, by planting seeds of positivity and using language that upholds our aspirations, we create a fertile ground for growth and achievement.

The relationship between thought, language, and reality is supported by a wealth of research demonstrating that positive thinking and affirmative speech can lead to improved outcomes in various aspects of life, including health, relationships, and career success. This underscores the importance of being mindful of our internal dialogue and the conversations we engage in. By aligning our thoughts and words with our desired outcomes, we harness the power to steer our lives in the direction of our aspirations.

Moreover, this principle acts as a foundational element in the practice of Extreme Dialogue. It emphasizes the significance of intentional thought and speech as tools for shaping our reality. Through self-reflection and purposeful conversation, we not only uncover deeper insights into our desires and barriers but also activate the potential to transform these insights into tangible success.

In essence, recognizing the foundational role of thoughts and language in shaping our reality marks the first step towards transforming our dreams into achievements.

Employ Intentional, Data-informed Conversations for Personal and Professional Growth

Intentional, data-informed conversations serve as a bridge between where we currently stand and where we aspire to be. These are not mere exchanges of ideas; they are strategic dialogues informed by evidence and aimed at fostering personal and professional growth. The premise here is simple yet profound: informed discussions lead to informed decisions, which, in turn, lead to successful outcomes.

Imagine navigating a ship through unchartered waters. Without a map, the journey is based on guesswork, fraught with avoidable risks. Similarly, progressing in life without data is like sailing without a compass—possible but perilous. Data sheds light on patterns, trends, and insights that guide our conversations and decisions, much like a map guides a sailor, reducing the uncertainty inherent in the pursuit of success.

Employing data in our conversations requires a shift in mindset. It involves moving beyond anecdotal evidence and embracing quantitative and qualitative data. This approach empowers us with a clearer understanding of our situation, enables us to set realistic goals, and crafts strategies that are both achievable and measurable. Whether it's personal growth or professional development, data not only illuminates the path forward but also helps monitor progress and make necessary adjustments along the way.

This methodology aligns with the practices endorsed by Extreme Dialogue. By anchoring our conversations in data, we prioritize objectivity and clarity, avoiding the pitfalls of baseless assumptions. This data-driven dialogue fosters an environment where informed decisions flourish, paving the way for sustained growth and achievement.

Incorporating a data-informed perspective into our interactions enriches conversations, making them more meaningful and outcome-focused. But it raises an important question: Are we prepared to let data guide our dialogues, transforming the way we conceive our path to success?

Embrace the Transformative Power of Extreme Dialogue in the Digital Age, Moving from Abstract Dreams to Tangible Achievements

In an era where digital platforms have become the primary medium for communication, the principles of Extreme Dialogue have never been more relevant. This methodology extends beyond traditional discourse, advocating for a blend of intentional conversation and data analytics, empowering individuals to transform abstract dreams into tangible achievements.

Consider the process of sculpting. Just as a sculptor uses their tools to give form to a block of marble, Extreme Dialogue equips you with the necessary tools to carve out your desired reality from the myriad possibilities that the digital age presents. The sculptor's vision for the final piece guides each stroke, much like how a clear understanding of one's goals shapes the conversations and actions one undertakes.

The digital age amplifies the potential of Extreme Dialogue, providing access to a vast amount of data at our fingertips. From social media analytics to online market research, the digital realm offers insights that were once beyond reach, allowing for conversations that are not only intentional but deeply informed by empirical evidence. This integration of dialogue with digital analytics enables us to navigate our personal and professional paths with unprecedented precision and effectiveness.

Moreover, the digital era presents unique opportunities for collaboration and networking. Extreme Dialogue leverages these digital platforms to foster connections and engage in meaningful conversations with individuals across the globe. This global exchange of ideas and experiences enriches our perspectives, further enhancing the process of manifesting our aspirations into reality.

By embracing Extreme Dialogue in the digital age, we employ a methodology that uniquely combines intentionality, data, and the power of digital platforms, guiding us from the realm of dreams into the reality of accomplishments.

Through recognizing the role of thoughts and language, employing data-informed conversations, and embracing Extreme Dialogue's transformative power, we unlock the potential to craft our desired reality.

In mastering the art of Extreme Dialogue, you hold the key to

unlocking the potential within yourself and shaping the reality you desire. By recognizing the pivotal role of thoughts and language in crafting your personal reality, you pave the way for intentional, data-informed conversations that propel you towards growth and success. **Embrace the transformative power of Extreme Dialogue in the digital age,** where abstract dreams can be transformed into tangible achievements through deliberate dialogue with yourself and others. **By merging mindset with data analysis, Extreme Dialogue offers you a fresh perspective on manifesting your aspirations into concrete outcomes.**

Through intentional, data-informed conversations, you have the opportunity to bridge the gap between a positive mindset and real-world achievements. **Embrace the power of these conversations to shape your reality,** both personally and professionally, with a strategic approach that combines mindset techniques and empirical insights. **Forge genuine connections and transparent communication,** recognizing the importance of collaboration and trust in the journey towards tangible success.

As you embark on this transformative journey, remember that innovation and creativity play vital roles in realizing your goals. **Stay curious, think beyond boundaries,** and leverage the tools of Extreme Dialogue to manifest your aspirations in ways you never thought possible. With a focused mindset, data-driven strategies, and a commitment to authentic communication, you have the power to turn your dreams into tangible wins.

Keep the momentum going, and let each conversation, each reflection, and each action propel you closer to your dreams. In the realm of Extreme Dialogue, where thoughts become reality and language shapes outcomes, you have the agency to redefine your path and actualize your fullest potential. **The journey from dialogue to reality is yours to claim—step into it boldly and watch as your world transforms before your eyes.**

EPILOGUE

The Gateway to Tangible Triumph

As we draw the curtain on this transformative journey, it's essential to reflect on the pivotal moments and revelations that have led us here. The path from dialogue to reality is not merely a concept but a tangible process that keys into unlocking your utmost potential and driving meaningful outcomes in both your personal and professional life.

Real-world applications of the strategies and insights shared within these pages are vast and variegated. Whether you're steering a groundbreaking startup to new heights, orchestrating a brand's narrative to captivate a global audience, or simply nurturing personal relationships that foster mutual growth and understanding, the principles of Extreme Dialogue can be your compass.

Recollect, Reflect, and React

We delved into the depths of **data-informed decision-making**, asserting its unparalleled power in crafting strategies that resonate on a personal level and drive action. The discourse on **authentic communication** underscored the quintessence of building genuine connections, fostering an environment of trust and transparency that propels both individuals and organizations forward. Through **innovative thinking and creativity**, we navigated the landscapes of possibility, learning to see challenges not as roadblocks but as stepping-stones to greatness.

From Insight to Action

But insights, regardless of their depth, demand action to catalyze change. I encourage you to take the leap from understanding to implementation. Engage in **Extreme Dialogue** within your teams, with your audience, and importantly, with yourself. Reflect on your core values, aspirations, and the impact you wish to create. Use the data and feedback loops not as mere metrics but as narratives that guide your decisions, strategies, and actions.

Embrace Limitations as Launchpads

Acknowledging the limits of any methodology, including ours, is crucial. The landscapes of personal growth and professional success are ever-evolving; what works today may need reevaluation tomorrow. Hence, the journey with Extreme Dialogue is not a one-off but a continuous process of learning, adapting, and innovating. Your feedback, experiences, and stories are the nourishment that keeps this methodology alive and relevant.

The Call to Action

Armed with newfound knowledge and strategies, seize the day with boldness and confidence. Transform your aspirations into tangible achievements. Remember, the difference between dreaming and realizing is the courage to pursue the dialogue with commitment, resilience, and an unwavering belief in one's capacity for greatness.

Let this book not merely be a read but a blueprint for action. Let each day be a canvas for your art of manifestation, painted with the vibrant colors of aspiration, strategy, and tangible success.

A Lasting Impression

In closing, remember that your reality is not a product of chance but a masterpiece you sculpt with the chisel of Extreme Dialogue. Each word you utter, every strategy you implement, and every connection you nurture adds a stroke to this masterpiece.

As you forge ahead, carry with you the conviction that **your words have the power to shape your world**. Let this knowledge not just dwell in the confines of these pages but breathe life into your every endeavor.

"The only limit to our realization of tomorrow will be our doubts of today." - Franklin D. Roosevelt

Let's erase those doubts with bold dialogues and transform today's visions into tomorrow's realities.

www.ingramcontent.com/pod-product-compliance
Lightning Source LLC
Chambersburg PA
CBHW071059240526
45471CB00016B/2160